D1597187

ART OF THE

MUSCLE CAR

DAVID NEWHARDT · PETER HARHOLDT

motorbooks

First published in 2009 by Motorbooks, an imprint of MBI Publishing Company, 400 First Avenue North, Suite 300, Minneapolis, MN, 55401 USA

Copyright © 2009 by MBI Publishing Company and Peter Harholdt

All rights reserved. With the exception of quoting brief passages for the purposes of review, no part of this publication may be reproduced without prior written permission from the Publisher.

The information in this book is true and complete to the best of our knowledge. All recommendations are made without any guarantee on the part of the author or Publisher, who also disclaim any liability incurred in connection with the use of this data or specific details.

We recognize, further, that some words, model names, and designations mentioned herein are the property of the trademark holder. We use them for identification purposes only. This is not an official publication.

MBI Publishing Company titles are also available at discounts in bulk quantity for industrial or sales-promotional use. For details write to Special Sales Manager at MBI Publishing Company, 400 First Avenue North, Suite 300, Minneapolis, MN, 55401 USA

Library of Congress Cataloging-in-Publication Data

Newhardt, David, 1955-
   Art of the muscle car / David Newhardt ; photographs by Peter Harholdt.
      p. cm.
   ISBN-13: 978-0-7603-3591-8
   1. Muscle cars—United States—History—20th century.
   2. Muscle cars—United States—Pictorial works. I. Harholdt, Peter. II. Title.
   TL23.N484 2009
   629.222—dc22

                                        2009014122

On the cover: 1970 Boss 429 Mustang.

On the frontispiece: 1969 Dodge Charger 500 fuel cap.

On the title page: 1969 Chevrolet El Camino SS 396 *and* 1967 Dodge Charger Hemi.

About the author

Photographer and writer David Newhardt was born in Chicago, Illinois, and attended Southern Illinois University majoring in professional photography. He served eight years in the US Navy aboard nuclear submarines before settling in Southern California. Newhardt worked at *Motor Trend* for three years and has been on the mastheads of many automotive magazines. He has worked in the fashion photography field but finds automobiles easier to deal with. The author of seven books, Newhardt has supplied scores of other books with images. A long-time member of the Motor Press Guild, he is married and has two sons. Newhardt lives in Pasadena, California.

About the Photographer

Peter Harholdt is a lifelong car enthusiast, SCCA racer, and preeminent studio photographer. He has been entrusted to photograph countless priceless works of art for museums and exhibit catalogs. He first developed his portable studio to create the stunning hot rod portraits featured in Motorbooks' *Art of the Hot Rod*. Harholdt lives in West Palm Beach, Florida.

Editor: Darwin Holmstrom
Designer: Chris Fayers
Cover design: John Barnet/4Eyes Design

Printed in China

CONTENTS

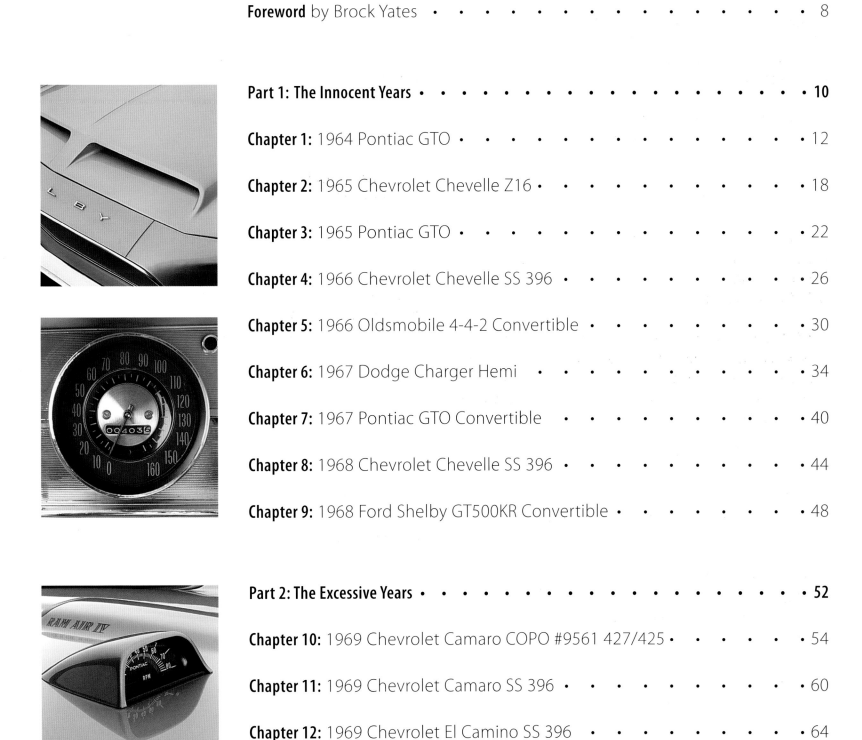

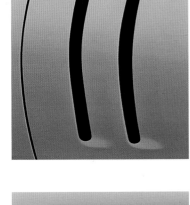

FOREWORD

by Brock Yates

A wet dream on wheels . . . that's what a muscle car is. The embodiment of every adolescent and adult male's hopes and dreams. The tool by which scores were settled, reputations made, and social outcasts embraced. By tapping into the imagination and buying power of the baby boomer generation, the muscle cars of the 1960s and '70s redefined our culture.

The country was heady with the taste of freedom upon emerging from the Great Depression and World War II, flush with disposable income, and raucously in need of speed. As the era of the hot rod was winding down and the NHRA, with Wally Parks at the helm, was turning drag racing from a sport into an entertainment event, the American auto industry was working to fill a void in the marketplace.

Throughout the 1950s automobiles began to change from comfortable modes of transportation to symbols of angst and independence. The inception of the big-block V-8 engine changed American automobiles. GM, with help from John Delorean, set off a powder keg of inspiration and competition when it introduced the Pontiac GTO to the American market.

These relatively inexpensive beasts were readily available, could be souped up in countless ways, and created a generation of "race 'em on Sunday, sell 'em on Monday" drivers who lived by the adage I hold near and dear: "The only rule is there are no rules!"

Photo by Steve Rossin

The burgeoning racing scene in L.A. and on Detroit's Woodward Avenue was changing everything, and the Big Three were scrambling to keep up with the ever-increasing sales of muscle cars. At *Car and Driver*, we had a front-row seat to changes taking place within the industry, and Detroit threw open its doors to grant us unheralded access to new models coming out of the factories.

One of the most brilliant marketing moves I ever saw was the hyped-up race between the Pontiac GTO and Ferrari. The reality was a showroom-floor Pontiac couldn't beat Ferrari, but the buying public wasn't aware of this. Unbeknownst to Ferrari and *Car and Driver*, Royal Pontiac, a race shop masquerading as a dealership, provided an aftermarket high-performance Pontiac GTO for the test, and history was made. Through a Herculean and underhanded effort, Pontiac beat Ferrari, and thus began the greatest word-of-mouth marketing campaign ever run in this country.

With an ever-increasing market share and bands like the Beach Boys touting the merits of the 409, muscle cars were here to stay . . . or, so we thought. A mere decade would pass before this purely American phenomenon would face a confluence of outside forces bent on regulating every aspect of the auto industry, undermining the viability and vitality of muscle cars in the process.

By the early seventies, Ralph Nader and his merry band of buffoons were in full cry, and federal restrictions were being enacted against automakers. In reaction to more restrictive safety legislation, the Cannonball/Sea to Shining Sea/Memorial Trophy Dash was created, and in honor of this race, I purchased the love of my life, a white 1971 Dodge Challenger that I had rebuilt by legendary stock-car racer Cotton Owens. This car uses a modified 340-cubic-inch V-8, carries 55 gallons of fuel, and has a roll bar, Recaro seats, special suspension, and a tall 2.76 final gear for high-speed, coast-to-coast highway travel. This beauty still sits in my garage and is the cornerstone of my small, but beloved, car collection.

By 1974 the writing was on the wall. The Clean Air Act, Draconian insurance practices, OPEC's oil embargo, and the threat of depleted oil reserves destroyed the market for muscle cars in America. The Pontiac GTO brought us into the era, and the Pontiac Super Duty ended it.

While the era had ended, the dreams never died. The Pontiac GTO, Chevrolet Chevelle and Camaro, Plymouth 'Cuda, Dodge Charger and Challenger, and Ford Mustang still get gearheads cranked. The throaty growl of a high-performance engine still engenders fantasies. Almost 30 years later, modern versions of these masterpieces are being reintroduced to a new generation of drivers, but it's a new world.

These reproductions of original muscle cars are hot, but they don't engender the same passion they once did. They are faster, sleeker, and safer than their ancestors, but they are expensive, and you can't tinker with 'em. Computers have all but destroyed a layman's ability to toil under the hood, and while street racing is making a comeback, these races showcase smaller, lighter cars, not the heavy behemoths of our youth. The adage "You can never go home again" is true. We will never truly revisit the decade of the muscle car, but boy, what a ride we had.

Bruce Yates

Part 1

THE INNOCENT YEARS

John Z. DeLorean commissioned his engineers to build the very first muscle car—Pontiac's GTO—because General Motors had ordered Pontiac to cease its racing efforts, efforts that had taken Pontiac from a struggling division to the number three brand in the United States, behind only Chevrolet and Ford. The GTO, which was really a gussied up Le Mans midsize sedan with a big, fast engine, turned out to be exactly the right catalyst injected into U.S. culture at exactly the right time to ignite a performance-car era the likes of which had never been seen before. And will never be seen again. No one quite knew what was happening at the time, or the extremes the muscle-car phenomenon would eventually reach, but everyone knew that the GTO was spot-on perfect for the exploding baby-boom market. It was a simple car with a big engine, and 1964 America was a simple place (though that would soon change), a country dissected by a highway system that opened up virtually any possibility a person taking to those roads could imagine. And the amazing new muscle cars coming out of Detroit were just the rides to carry those young dreamers to unlimited horizons.

Chapter 1

1964 PONTIAC GTO

For everything, there is a first. While many may argue that the "muscle car" started in the 1950s with the Chrysler 300, or even before that with the Olds Rocket 88, the birth of the muscle car, according to the classic formula—a huge engine in a midsize platform—occurred with the release of Pontiac's GTO. The GTO, an option package that consisted of a handful of emblems and a healthy 389-cubic-inch V-8 mounted on and in the upscale Le Mans version of the division's then-new Tempest, the GTO revolutionized the performance car market.

The GTO was a massive success not only because of its tire-shredding performance but also because of Pontiac's superb marketing efforts, spearheaded by ad exec and drag racer Jim Wangers. By targeting his marketing efforts at the young and young-at-heart, Wangers' promotional work made the GTO a virtual icon overnight. (It helped that the car could trounce virtually any other car fresh off a dealer's showroom floor.)

In perhaps his most audacious marketing move, Wangers arranged for *Car and Driver* magazine to pit the Pontiac GTO against the famous Ferrari GTO, at least on paper. You see, the magazine couldn't get its hands on an example of the Ferrari at the same time it had Pontiac GTOs on hand for testing, so a cover painting was used in lieu of an actual head-to-head shootout photo. Yet, at the end of the day, the Pontiac acquitted itself very well against the vaunted Italian sports car. Partly it may have been because Wangers had covertly swapped a hot-rodded Pontiac 421-cubic-inch engine in place of the stock 389-cubic-inch unit. In any case, the resulting tidal wave of power blew the *Car and Driver* testers away.

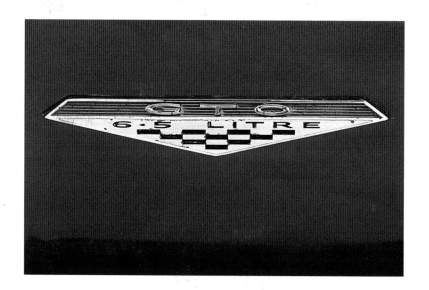

The Pontiac GTO exceeded all expectations. While some might have felt that 32,450 units sold wasn't a success, in truth Pontiac hadn't expected to move anywhere near that number. Better yet was the halo effect the hot new Pontiac provided. It seemed that every magazine had considerable coverage of the new model, and it drew significant traffic into Pontiac showrooms. It didn't take long for every manufacturer in Detroit to sit up and take notice. Their responses to the GTO resulted in the biggest horsepower race in automotive history. And the GTO was there first.

Base engine: 389-cubic-inch V-8, 325 horsepower, 428 lbs-ft of torque
Base price: $3,377.91
Curb weight: 3,126 lbs
Production numbers: 7,384 coupes; 18,422 hardtops; 6,644 convertibles
Number produced with base engine: 24,205

1964 PONTIAC GTO

Chapter 2

1965 CHEVROLET CHEVELLE Z16

The introduction of Pontiac's GTO in 1964 left the public clamoring for muscle cars from all of the manufacturers, and Chevrolet sure wasn't going to be left out of the fledgling market. The Bow Tie division had the midsize Chevelle Malibu, built on the same corporate architecture as Pontiac's GTO. By using the stout convertible frame beneath a closed body, front and rear anti-roll bars, and a beefed-up front suspension, Chevy engineers had an ideal repository for the Mark IV 396-cubic-inch V-8. Rated at 375 horsepower, the RPO L78 big-block was only available with a Muncie four-speed manual transmission (the 420 lbs-ft of torque generated by the L78 would have mulched Chevrolet's antiquated two-speed Powerglide automatic transmission), with power flowing through a huge 11-inch clutch. This powerplant featured specifications virtually identical to those found in the 396-cubic-inch L78 mill installed in the Corvette, except that in the Corvette the engine was rated at 425 horsepower. This likely had more to do with corporate politics than with any technical differences between the engines.

The exterior was the polar opposite of the maelstrom beneath the hood: a single Malibu SS 396 badge on the rear and a pair of crossed flags and engine call-outs on the front fenders were the only clues that this car was a purpose-built drag machine with a license plate. The interior was standard Malibu, a comfortable mix of style and space. The only hint of the reprehensible behavior of which this car was capable was a 160-mile-per-hour speedometer mounted in the instrument panel. While nobody was really expecting the Z16 to peg the speedo, it could cover the quarter-mile in the 14-second range, an especially impressive feat considering the lack of grip produced by the bias-ply tires of the day.

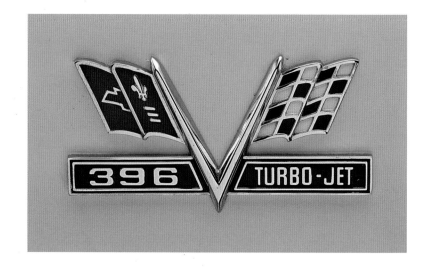

Chevrolet didn't exactly advertise the Z16. It was a stopgap effort intended to counter the GTO, and GM's marketing types were still trying to keep the new breed of outlaw muscle cars under the radar. The Z16 wasn't cost effective to build, so Chevy limited production, building just 201 examples, including this Crocus Yellow vehicle with a black top. Only 10 Z16s left the factory with this color combination. Two other colors were offered: Tuxedo Black and Regal Red. The Z16 lasted just one year and was replaced by the Chevelle SS 396 for the 1966 model year.

Base engine: 396 cubic inches, 375 horsepower, 420 lbs-ft of torque

Base price: $4,091.00

Price of Z16 option: $1,501.05

Curb weight: 3,600 lbs

Production numbers: 200 coupes; 1 convertible

Number produced with engine: 201

1965 CHEVROLET CHEVELLE Z16

Chapter 3

1965 PONTIAC GTO

In its sophomore year, Pontiac cloaked the GTO in new sheet metal. While the 115-inch wheelbase didn't change, the overall vehicle length increased 3 inches. Vertically stacked headlights and a full-width grill gave the GTO a buff, muscular look, reflecting the division's Wide-Track look. Under the huge hood lurked a 389-cubic-inch V-8, available in one of two flavors: a 335-horsepower version equipped with a single four-barrel carburetor, and an optional Tri-Power version rated at 360 horses. Either engine delivered plenty of grunt: the base engine could vault the GTO to 60 miles per hour in just 7.2 seconds, while the quarter-mile was dispatched in only 16.1 seconds at 89 miles per hour.

When the GTO debuted in 1964, it rolled onto the showroom as a mid-year entry. This limited sales, but by the time the '65 GTO hit dealer lots, Pontiac was ready to sell its muscle car in significant volumes. An advertising blitz, including the release of a 45-rpm record that allowed aspiring GTO owners to hear their favorite car being put through its paces, was hitting its stride. A convertible version was even tapped for pace car duties at the 1965 *Motor Trend* Riverside 500 race.

Yet not every muscle car led a pampered life; witness this example. Converted to a race car upon initial purchase, it spent its formative years hammering down various drag strips. While that lifestyle tended to keep the miles low, each click of the odometer was hard fought. Finally, this GTO was pulled from front-line duty and converted back into a street car, a conversion that included the installation of a new white interior.

Base engine: 389-cubic-inch V-8, 335 horsepower, 431 lbs-ft of torque

Base price: $2,855.00

Price of GTO option: $295.90

Curb weight: 3,478 lbs

Production numbers: 8,319 coupes; 55,722 hardtops; 11,311 convertibles

Chapter 4

1966 CHEVROLET CHEVELLE SS 396

The Chevelle was growing up in 1966, displaying new curves and exhibiting bolder behavior. The voluptuous contours came courtesy of fresh sheet metal for '66, while the big-block engine provided plenty of opportunity for an owner to express his or her inner hooligan. For the 1966 model year Chevrolet took the wraps off an A-body platform that had a more aggressive look than its predecessor, with a forward-leaning grill and sweeping C-pillars. Rather than offering the SS model as a mere option group, Chevrolet made the Chevelle SS a separate member of the Chevelle line for 1966. The Bow Tie division had begun taking performance very seriously; performance, both real and perceived, sold cars.

Two faux louvers adorned the top of the broad hood of the SS 396 Chevelle, but there was nothing artificial under the hood. Big-block muscle, and lots of it, ensured that a driver with a heavy foot could make short work of a set of rear tires. A trio of 396 engines meant that a buyer could get as much horsepower as he or she wanted, or could afford. The standard SS 396 powerplant—RPO L35—generated 325 horsepower and boasted 410 lbs-ft of torque. The next rung up the ladder to performance excess was RPO L34, which used components like a forged crankshaft, four-bolt main bearing caps, and an aggressive camshaft to help deliver 360 horses and 420 lbs-ft of twist. At the top of the 396 food chain resided RPO L78, an engine with increased compression, solid-valve lifters, and an even hotter bumpstick, all in the pursuit of 375 horsepower and 415 lbs-ft of torque. This

engine could hurl a Chevelle to 60 miles per hour in just 6.5 seconds. That kind of performance put the Chevelle in the thick of stoplight battles on any Saturday night. And let's not kid ourselves, the Chevelle SS was built to cover a straight line very quickly. Anything else was just gravy.

Base engine: 396 cubic inches, 325 horsepower, 410 lbs-ft of torque
Base price: $2,276.00
Curb weight: 3,375 lbs
Production numbers: 72,272 (includes both hardtops and convertibles)

1966 CHEVROLET CHEVELLE SS 396

Chapter 5

1966 OLDSMOBILE 4-4-2 CONVERTIBLE

Not every muscle car devotee wanted a bare bones vehicle that delivered a large dose of performance with a miniscule dollop of comfort. For the buyer who wanted it all—gut-wrenching acceleration, acceptable handling, and luxurious surroundings—the list of potential muscle cars was very short. And at the top of the page was Oldsmobile's 4-4-2.

Oldsmobile offered the 4-4-2 package in five body types, including the Cutlass Sport Coupe, Cutlass Holiday Coupe, Club Coupe, Deluxe Holiday Coupe, and Cutlass Convertible. The 4-4-2 option started with the 1964 model and was actually the civilian version of the B09 Police Apprehender Pursuit package. Before long, the public embraced the 4-4-2 as a viable alternative in the muscle-car field.

While some muscle cars packed more cubic inches and horsepower beneath their hoods than the brawny Oldsmobile, the 4-4-2 didn't have to extend any apologies. With 400 cubic inches of V-8, the base 4-4-2 was rated at 350 horsepower. Midway through the model year Oldsmobile released the RPO L69 option, putting a Tri-Power induction system on the powerplant. This setup checked in with 360 ponies, enough for *Car Life* magazine to flog a 4-4-2 up to 60 miles per hour in only 6.3 seconds. The drag strip could be covered in 15.2 seconds at 96.6 miles per hour, respectable for a full-size vehicle with bias-ply tires.

Of all of the 4-4-2 models offered in 1966, the rarest was the convertible. The 4-4-2 convertible exuded a level of sophistication unheard of in most muscle cars. Compared to its competition, it was a gentleman's express among a pack of hooligans.

Base engine: 400 cubic inches, 350 horsepower, 440 lbs-ft of torque

Horsepower and torque for this car: 360 horsepower, 440 lbs-ft of torque

Base price: $2,965.00

Curb weight: 3,629 lbs

Production numbers: 2,129 (L69)

Number produced with this engine: 240 (convertibles)

1966 OLDSMOBILE 4-4-2 CONVERTIBLE

1966 OLDSMOBILE 4-4-2 CONVERTIBLE

Chapter 6

1967 DODGE CHARGER HEMI

Debuting in 1966 as a competitor to the midsize offerings from General Motors, the Charger was essentially a B-body Dodge Coronet with a fastback design, at that time a popular styling feature. Available with a wide range of engines, the top-shelf powerplant was the famed 426 Hemi. In its sophomore year, the Charger continued to utilize the race-inspired engine to trounce stoplight challenges. This Charger, the first one equipped with a Hemi for 1967, was a well-appointed cruiser, distinctly different than the Mopar muscle cars that would roll onto the street in the coming years.

Much has been written about the 426 street Hemi, claiming that it was an oil-burning, cold-blooded, temperamental engine. In fact, a well-maintained Hemi no more needed special treatment than any other high-performance engine. Under low-rpm driving, the spark plugs would tend to foul, but a flexing of the accelerator would clear the electrodes, with the resulting sprint down the quarter-mile only requiring 14.4 seconds at 100 miles per hour. Never a cheap option, the $877.55 Hemi did little for a vehicle's cornering ability, but then one didn't buy a Hemi to slalom. Being a race-derived powerplant, the 426 Hemi lived for the upper range of the tachometer. Off the line, lesser engines in the Mopar lineup, such as the 440, would grab the lead on the Hemi, but as speeds increased, the top-end strength of the 426 came to the fore, hurling

the Hemi down the road. The sound of a Hemi at full throttle will give anyone goose bumps, and that's one of the most appealing features of the car. Unfortunately, it didn't appeal to many buyers; only 118 were equipped with the Hemi for 1967. Today, they're some of the rarest muscle cars around.

Base engine: 318-cubic-inch V-8, 230 horsepower, 340 lbs-ft of torque
Optional engines: 383-cubic-inch V-8, 326 horsepower, 400 lbs-ft of torque; 440-cubic-inch V-8, 375 horsepower, 480 lbs-ft of torque; 426-cubic-inch Hemi V-8, 425 horsepower, 490 lbs ft of torque
Base price: $3,128
Price of Hemi engine option: $877.55
Curb weight: 3,480 lbs
Production numbers: 15,788
Number produced with this engine: 118

1967 DODGE CHARGER HEMI

1967 DODGE CHARGER HEMI

Chapter 7

1967 PONTIAC GTO CONVERTIBLE

As the decade of the 1960s began to wind down, Pontiac continued to refine the popular GTO. Subtle exterior trim changes and minor updates with the interior were what most people noticed for the 1967 model year. Yet beneath the hood, changes were bolder. No longer was a Tri-Power induction system available, thanks to an edict from GM's corporate management. To compensate, the 389-cubic-inch V-8 grew, courtesy of a bore-out, to 400 cubes. Pontiac found that the pricey Tri-Power option, while a marvel to look at, was an expensive route to horsepower. The Wide-Track division found better living through cubic inches. It was cheaper and easier to deliver massive amounts of power just by enlarging the engine. Four flavors of 400-cubic-inch fun were on the menu, and while some sprang for the "Economy" version of the engine, the vast majority of buyers were content with the stomping base 400, with its 335 horsepower and axle-twisting 441 lbs-ft of torque.

A small number of the GTOs of this era were "massaged" by the top wrench at Royal Pontiac, in Royal Oak, Michigan. This dealership marketed and sold a performance-enhancing package for GTOs that included thinner head gaskets, recurved distributors, colder spark plugs, larger jets in the carburetor, and a bunch more performance tweaks. The resulting "Royal Bobcat" was a street-legal vehicle that produced startling power. Exterior indications of Royal's work were held to a minimum, the better to reel in unsuspecting drivers.

One dealer option that turned heads was the forged-aluminum Hurst wheels. Hurst had a well-earned reputation for unbreakable products, and these wheels were no different. The only problem was the cost: $69.50 per wheel, big money in 1967. But nobody argued that they didn't look great on a GTO, especially on a convertible.

Base engine: 400 cubic inches, 335 horsepower, 441 lbs-ft of torque
Base price: $3,165.00
Curb weight: 3,515 lbs
Production numbers: 9,517

1967 PONTIAC GTO CONVERTIBLE

RAM AIR

Chapter 8

1968 CHEVROLET CHEVELLE SS 396

Chevrolet made sure that any vehicle in its lineup wearing the Super Sport badge had the beans to back up its aggressive looks. Chevy introduced a new body on the popular Chevelle in 1968, and the svelte shape took well to the SS treatment. With the Mark IV big-block engine under the hood, the Chevelle was a dangerous foe at a stoplight. Three levels of 396 performance were offered, with horsepower ranging from 325 to 375.

But there is always somebody who wants more, especially when it comes to performance. Chevrolet had developed a set of aluminum heads to bolt onto the RPO L78 396, reducing weight over the front wheels by about 200 pounds. Released for sale in December of 1967, and using the RPO code of L89, these limited-production heads were temperamental, producing popping and spitting until the aluminum warmed up and expanded, sealing the combustion chambers. But they flowed well, and with a solid-lifter valvetrain, 11.0:1 compression, and a huge 800cfm Holley carburetor, they helped to generate a bit more than the factory-rated 375. It's believed that this car may be the last remaining example of a 1968 Chevelle SS 396 with RPO L89.

Of course, being a Super Sport, this Chevelle enjoyed a full slate of performance goodies, including dual exhaust, heavy-duty suspension, and badging inside and out. When people who knew a thing or two about performance pulled up next to a Chevelle, cocked an ear toward the engine compartment, and heard the "tappety-tappety" sound of solid lifters at work, they knew they'd better be packing some serious horsepower before challenging the potent Chevrolet. Once the big Holley was slammed open and

the engine started collecting revs like a hungry politician collects contributions at a fundraiser, an L89-equipped Chevy A-body would pick up and fly, charging to 60 miles per hour in just 6.5 seconds. If you kept the hammer down, the quarter-mile would fly by in 14.5 seconds at 100 miles per hour. And we wonder why the insurance companies started getting suspicious.

Base engine: 396 cubic inches, 325 horsepower, 410 lbs-ft of torque

Horsepower and torque for this car: 375 horsepower, 415 lbs-ft of torque

Base price: $2,899.00

Curb weight: 3,475 lbs

Production numbers: 62,785 (total Chevelle SS models built)

Chapter 9

1968 FORD SHELBY GT500KR CONVERTIBLE

When bench racers get together to swap lies, everyone agrees that top honor for cool car names goes to Carroll Shelby. From the Cobra to the GT500KR, the Texan had a knack for labeling his cars for maximum effect. The mouth-filling GT500KR, short for King of the Road, had the performance to match the name.

Understand, Shelby wasn't building race cars that could be driven on the street anymore. In fact, Ford was building the cars labeled Shelby by '68, but with heavy input from Carroll. Equipped with an R-code 428-cubic-inch Cobra Jet engine, the GT500KR was a very fast Grand Touring car rather than the tossable race car with lights that carried Shelby's name back in 1965. Ford released the hot big-block Cobra late in the model year, and Shelby, hearing that Chevrolet was planning to call a version of its big-block Camaro the King of the Road, beat Chevy to the punch by calling his latest road car the GT500KR.

By 1968, insurance companies were starting to sniff around factory muscle cars. Flaunting big numbers in a sales brochure was like waving a red flag, so Ford/Shelby rated the beefy Cobra Jet engine at just 335 horsepower. Sure, it made 335 horses, on its way to making yet more. The torque figure of 440 lbs-ft was closer to the real output of the huge V-8. The hood scoops weren't there for show; they fed cool ambient air directly into the air cleaner.

Since this was a Shelby, the suspension was not ignored. Ford fitted heavy-duty shock absorbers front and rear. On vehicles equipped with manual transmissions, the rear shocks were staggered in an attempt to minimize axle hop under heavy acceleration. With the Texas-sized torque of the Cobra Jet engine, the GT500KR was and still is good fodder for bench racers everywhere.

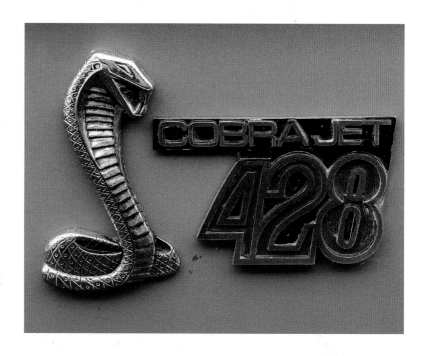

Base engine: 428 cubic inches, 335 horsepower, 440 lbs-ft of torque

Base price: $4,594.09

Curb weight: 3,200 lbs

Production numbers: 1,053 fastbacks; 517 convertibles

1968 FORD SHELBY GT500KR CONVERTIBLE

Part 2

THE EXCESSIVE YEARS

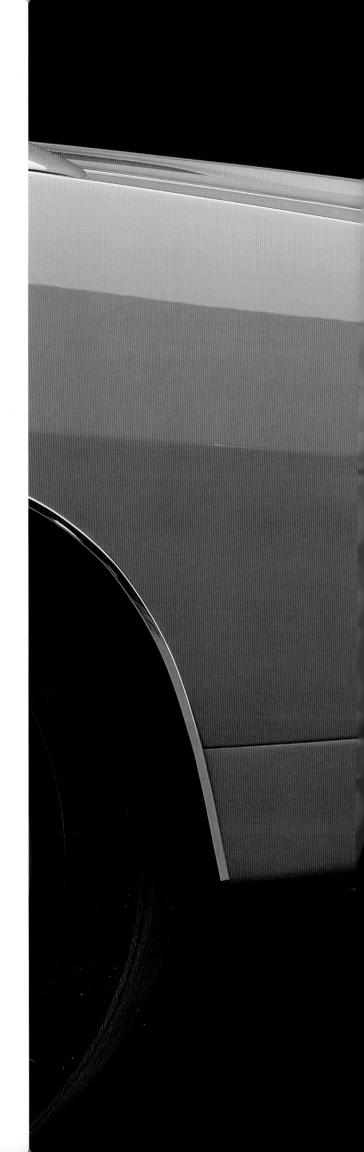

As the 1960s wound down, wretched excess defined every part of American culture: excessive drug use, excessive sex, excessive rock-and-roll lifestyles. The automotive industry was not immune; in fact, the excessive muscle cars Detroit produced during this period symbolize the hedonism of the era as much as Woodstock or the Summer of Love. Excessive or not, muscle cars of the late 1960s and early 1970s are spectacular creations, embodying the optimism, power, and dreams of a culture that knew no boundaries. Just as we'll never see the likes of Jimi Hendrix or Muhammad Ali again, so will we never see the likes of Chrysler's winged NASCAR racers for the street, the Dodge Daytona Charger and Plymouth Superbird. Nor will we see such brutish machinery as a Hemi 'Cuda, an LS6 Chevelle, a Super Cobra Jet Mustang, or a Buick GSX. While we can still buy cars that equal these fabled models in performance, we'll never see anything as pure and raw again. Perhaps this is a good thing; the excess of the period took a terrible toll on the baby boom generation. Unbridled drug use led to overdoses, promiscuous sex led to rampant venereal disease, and far too many inexperienced drivers ended their lives in overpowered, ill-handling muscle cars. But in sanitizing our culture—our lives as well as our cars—we've lost the sensation of being alive. Nothing can recapture that sensation, if even for just a brief moment, like a fast ride in a powerful muscle car.

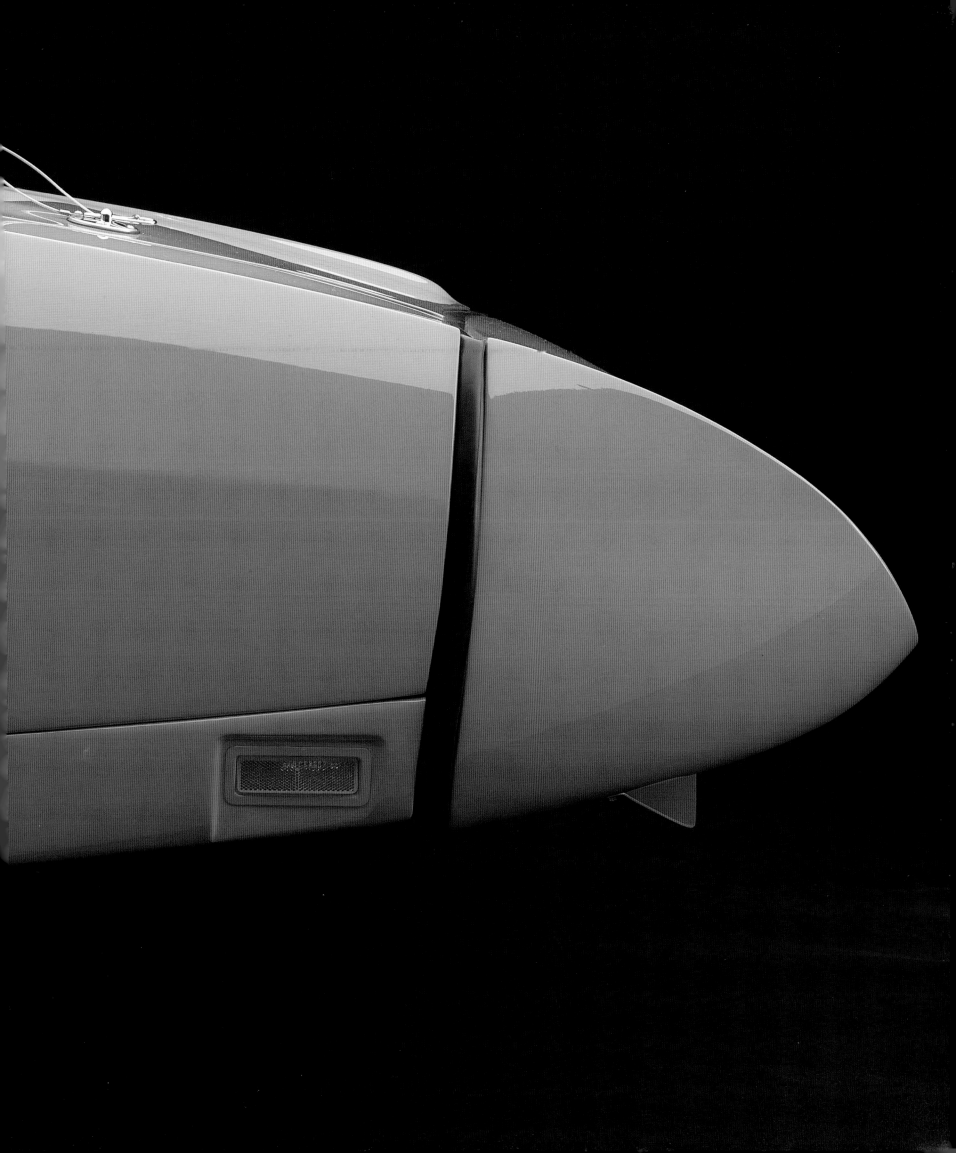

Chapter 10

1969 CHEVROLET CAMARO COPO #9561 427/425

Don Yenko, the performance-oriented Chevrolet dealer from Pennsylvania, had been slipping huge big-block engines into Camaros since the F-body's debut. Removing the old engine and installing a crate engine was a successful transplant, but it took considerable labor, as well as requiring the "disposal" of the original engine. So in June 1968, Yenko, long a personal friend of the executive suite at Chevrolet, asked the Bow Tie division to install the fierce 427-cubic-inch engine into the car at the factory. Chevrolet agreed, and soon knowledgeable dealers could use the Central Office Production Order system (COPO) to transform a healthy L78 396-engined Camaro into a very, very healthy L72 427.

Just over 1,000 Camaros were treated to the COPO package. There were three different COPOs offered: No. 9560, which got a buyer the famous ZL-1 427 aluminum-block race engine; No. 9737, the sports car conversion, which included a 140-mile-per-hour speedometer and chambered exhaust; and the package featured on this car, No. 9561, which was similar to the ZL-1 engine but used an iron block and came without transistor ignition. It featured the same massive power with just a bit more weight over the front wheels. Both four-speed manual and three-speed automatic transmissions were used, and either one would funnel stupid amounts of torque to the helpless rear tires.

Externally, there was little indication that a COPO Camaro was anything special. If anything, it looked like a stripper: dog-dish hubcaps and minimal badging, with just a cowl induction hood and a tail spoiler to give away the true nature of the car. Granted, anyone pulling up next to a COPO No. 9561–equipped Camaro would hear a lumpy idle, with each explosion in the cylinders audible. Then when the big Holley carburetor was slammed open, the explosions would blend into a snarling roar, the Camaro would hunt for traction, and then it would lunge toward the horizon.

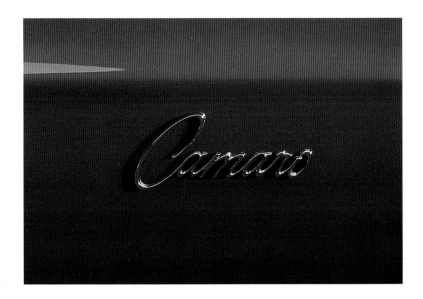

Base engine: 427-cubic-inch V-8, 425 horsepower, 450 lbs-ft of torque

Base price: $2,727.00

Price of COPO 9561 engine option: $489.75

Curb weight: 3,050 lbs

Production numbers: 1,015

Number produced with engine option: 1,015

1969 CHEVROLET CAMARO COPO #9561 427/425

Chapter 11

1969 CHEVROLET CAMARO SS 396

When Joe Q. Public walked into a Chevrolet dealership in 1969, if he was a gearhead, odds were good that this is the car in which he would be driving out. Built in relatively large numbers, and available at any Chevy house, a big-block-equipped Camaro was a potent package. Any Camaro equipped with a torque-heavy, L78, 396-cubic-inch engine, factory-rated at 375 horsepower, was an affordable ground-bound missile. A factory warranty just sweetened the deal.

In the race to get more horsepower into the hands of grateful drivers, Chevrolet pursued the same path to easy thrust as virtually every other manufacturer: better living through more cubic inches. It was child's play for Chevrolet engineers to install the division's proven 396-cubic-inch engine into the Camaro. With almost 60 percent of the vehicle weight over the front wheels, the Camaro SS 396 was a straight-line beast. Moderately priced, it was a performance steal. With the SS package, the Camaro was comfortably equipped, featuring a tasteful mixture of visual machismo and functional brutality. The rectangular-port iron heads, while heavy, flowed well, resulting in plenty of torque right off of idle. The Camaro SS 396 could reach 60 miles per hour in just 6.8 seconds and cover the quarter-mile in 14.7 seconds at 98.7 miles per hour. Axle hop under heavy acceleration was an issue, but most serious racers used aftermarket components to quell it.

In 1969 Chevrolet was serious about providing performance at every level, and the Camaro SS 396 was a real go-fast bargain. It didn't hurt that its halo spread across the entire Camaro line. Chevy liked to boast that there was a little SS in every Camaro. With the 396/375 engine, there was a lot.

Base engine: 396 cubic inches, 375 horsepower, 415 lbs-ft of torque
Base price: $3,100.00
Price of SS 396 option: $316.00
Curb weight: 3,790 lbs
Production numbers: 5,200
Number produced with this engine: 4,889

Chapter 12

1969 CHEVROLET EL CAMINO SS 396

One of the advantages of having a wide range of vehicles in Chevrolet's lineup was that the division could pluck one out of the line and transform it into something else at minimal cost. Chevrolet had done this when it raided the Chevelle line to create the El Camino, a car-based pickup truck designed to battle Ford's popular Ranchero. With its trucklike bed it was a versatile hauler, but from the B-pillar forward, it was an A-body Chevelle. In the case of the SS 396 version, the El Camino could haul more than just bales of hay and pool cleaning supplies.

Chevrolet had offered the big-block engine in El Caminos starting in 1966, but the iron-block bruiser reached new levels of excess in '69. The base 396 that year was rated at 325 horsepower, but as any muscle car enthusiast knows, more is always better.

For the 1969 model year the El Camino SS 396 could be had with RPO Z25. This meant that the El Camino received the brutal L78 396/375 powerplant. With the bed behind the seats, weight over the driven wheels was an issue, and axle hop under heavy acceleration was a very real concern. Yet most El Camino buyers weren't into drag racing. For many, the trucklet made a lifestyle statement: weekday goods hauler, weekend toy hauler. Many insurance companies didn't catch the 396-cubic-inch engine under the hood, resulting in lower premiums.

Being a truck, it wasn't really designed to cling to a corner like a leech, but with its low center of gravity, it could take a corner far better than a regular pickup. With the exception of a rear anti-roll bar, it used Super Sport underpinnings,

helping it stay relatively flat in turns. But its forte was moving in a straight line. The El Camino SS 396 has always flown under the muscle car radar, but that's changing as enthusiasts discover that it's a wolf in sheep's clothing.

Base engine: 396 cubic inches, 325 horseower, 415 lbs-ft of torque

Horsepower and torque for this car: 375 horsepower, 415 lbs-ft of torque

Base price: $2,723.00

Price of SS396 option: $347.60

Curb weight: 3,210 lbs

Production numbers: 48,385

1969 CHEVROLET EL CAMINO SS 396

1969 CHEVROLET EL CAMINO SS 396

Chapter 13

1969 CHARGER 500

Dodge had introduced its refreshed styling on the Charger in 1968, and the public ate it up to the tune of 96,100 units. A large part of Dodge's sales success was its presence on the NASCAR tracks, increasing the Charger's visibility. Unfortunately, what looked good in the showroom didn't work on the race course. The dramatic rear window set in a tunnel framed by the C-pillars did nothing for aerodynamics at triple-digit speeds. Neither did the recessed grille.

Dodge engineers found that increasing the top speed of the vehicle by just 5 miles per hour would require 85 more horsepower, or a 15 percent reduction in drag. The chances of extracting more than four score of horsepower were slim, so in late 1968, Dodge stylists took a '68 Charger and created the Charger 500 prototype, complete with flush rear window, wind deflectors on the A-pillars, and a grille and headlight cluster brought out level with the front bumper. The resulting car wasn't as visually graceful as the standard Charger, but Dodge was hungry for checkered flags. NASCAR rules required that at least 500 street-legal vehicles be made to qualify for competition, hence the 500 name. The standard engine was the capable 440-cubic-inch V-8, attached to either a four-speed manual or three-speed automatic transmission. Dodge contracted an aftermarket company in Detroit, Creative Industries, to convert standard 1969 Charger R/Ts to Charger 500s. At the end of the production run, 559 Charger 500s had been built, including approximately 50 equipped with the 426 Hemi engine.

In race trim, the Charger 500 could nudge 200 miles per hour, but Ford continued to rack up the victories at Dodge's expense. Dodge went back to the drawing board, hoping to come up with a winning design. That's another chapter . . .

Base engine: 440-cubic-inch V-8, 375 horsepower, 480 lbs-ft of torque

Optional engine: 426-cubic-inch V-8, 425 horsepower, 490 lbs-ft of torque

Base price: $3,860

Price of engine option: $648.20

Curb weight: 3,671 lbs

Production numbers: 392

Number produced with this engine: 52

1969 CHARGER 500

Chapter 14

1969 DODGE CHARGER DAYTONA

Following the Charger 500's lack of success on the racetrack, Dodge was desperate to coax more speed from its race cars. Aerodynamic drag was keeping the Charger from the winner's circle, so Dodge's engineers attacked the problem by thinking outside the box. Their result was *way* outside the box; it was a radical approach to easing the Charger through high-velocity air.

Attaching 18 inches of sloping nose to the front of the vehicle and affixing a rear spoiler tall enough to allow the trunk lid to open fully made the car slippery enough to power past the aerodynamic competition from Ford. The flush rear window first seen on the Charger 500 was retained, which, when combined with the unconventional body bits, helped reduce the Daytona's coefficient of drag to an impressive 0.29. Daytonas claimed the first four positions in the namesake Daytona 500 race, and when a winged car hit the Bonneville Salt Flats with Bobby Isaac behind the wheel, the wild-looking vehicle hit 217 miles per hour. This was a seriously fast car. During the 1969 and 1970 seasons, Daytonas took the checkered flag at five more Grand National races.

Creative Industries took Charger R/Ts and transformed them into Daytonas at its Detroit facility. NASCAR required that at least 500 units be produced, and when the dust settled, Dodge delivered 503 street cars to American customers, while an additional 40 went to Canada. The vast majority were fitted with 440-cubic-inch V-8s, rated at 375 horsepower. Seventy buyers ponied up for the brutal 426 Hemi, which was topped with a pair of Carter AFB four-barrel carburetors. Heavy-duty brakes and suspension were standard, since the intended area of operations had a propensity toward left turns. The only external indication on the street-Hemi-equipped Daytonas was a small badge on the side of the car that said "Hemi." It was easy to overlook it, since the outlandish aero aids drew most of the attention.

Base engine: 440-cubic-inch V-8, 375 horsepower, 480 lbs-ft of torque

Optional engine: 426-cubic-inch V-8, 425 horsepower, 490 lbs-ft of torque

Base price: $5,261

Price of Hemi engine option: $648.20

Curb weight: 3,740 lbs

Production numbers: 503

Number produced with this engine: 70

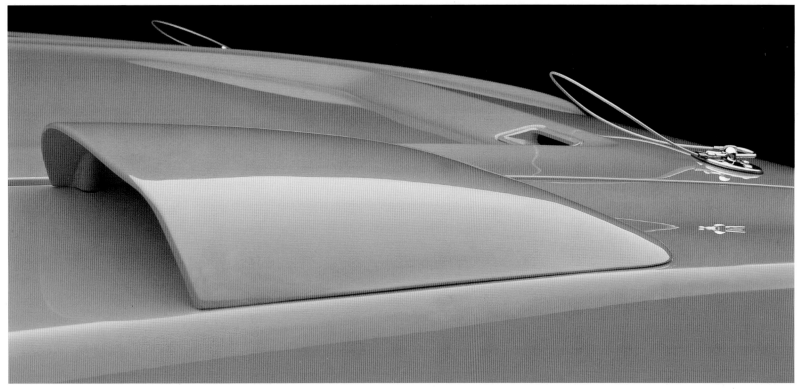

1969 DODGE CHARGER DAYTONA

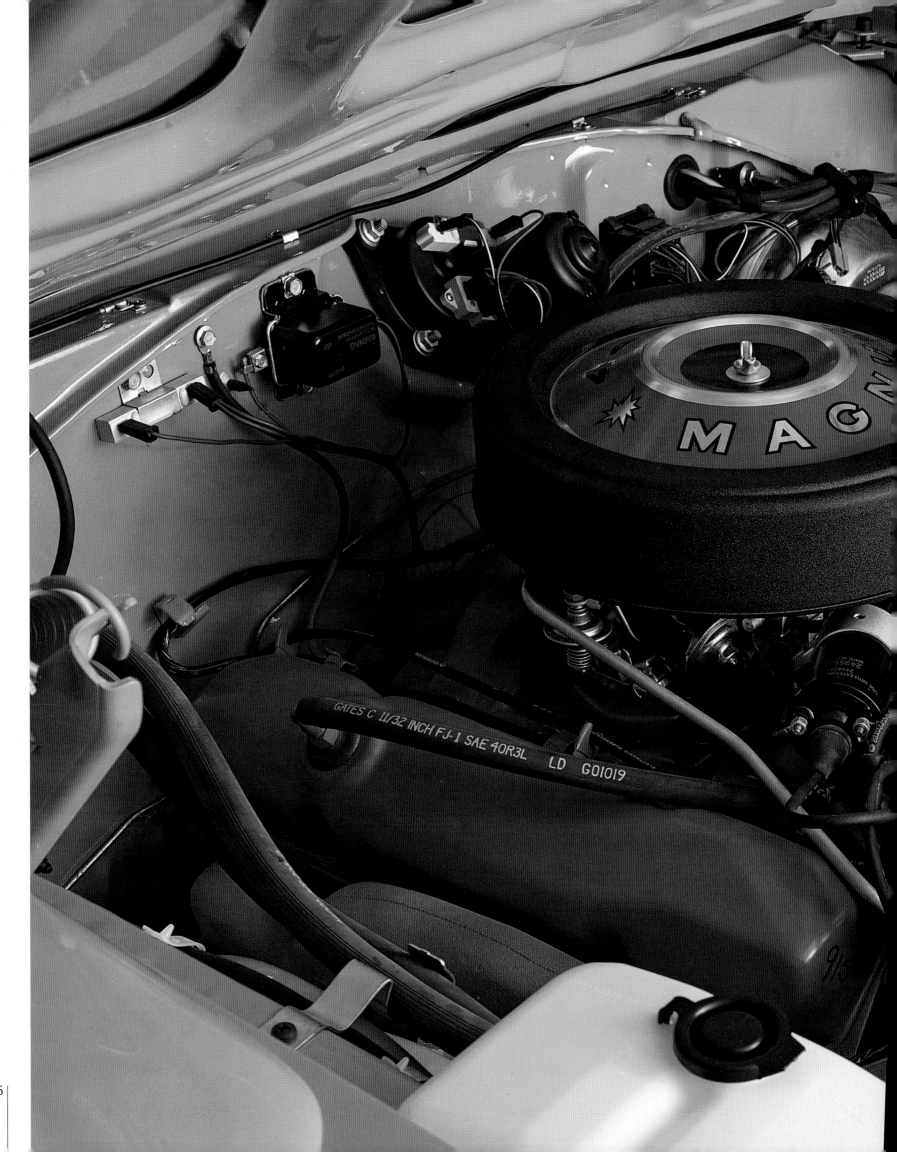

1969 DODGE CHARGER DAYTONA

Chapter 15

1969 DODGE SUPER BEE

Take a look at the classic muscle car formula (big engine in midsize platform) as the 1960s were drawing to a close, and you can see that the formula was being seriously diluted. Manufacturers were putting huge engines in almost everything in their lineups in an attempt to maximize sales to performance enthusiasts. But some of the results were less than stellar, while some were flat-out dogs.

But Dodge, long the working man's brand, stuck with simple cars with enormous, but simple, engines. Dodge showed that it could embrace the classic formula when it unveiled the Super Bee for 1969. Built on the B-body (see the name tie-in?), Dodge stuffed its 383-cubic-inch B-block mill in the engine room. The buyer of the car pictured shelled out for the huge optional 440-cubic-inch V-8, complete with Six-Pack induction system consisting of three two-barrel Holley carburetors and a lightweight, lift-off fiberglass hood. This was basic Muscle Car 101. The hood was fitted with a scoop large enough to ingest small children, and it was matte black, regardless of the vehicle color. Dog-dish hubcaps reinforced the image of low-cost performance. Inside were seats, a Hurst shifter, a steering wheel, and little else. What else does a real muscle car need?

How about brutal acceleration? The bargain-priced Super Bee could lunge to 60 miles per hour in 6.3 seconds, en route to covering the drag strip in 13.8 seconds at 104.2 miles per hour. It didn't hurt that Dodge fit the same suspension components on the Super Bee that it used on Hemi-powered cars. The result was a vehicle that could really get the power down a straight line.

Another key part of the classic muscle car formula was a decided inability to corner and stop. Here the Super Bee didn't disappoint, using drum brakes to subdue the velocity. But nobody bought a Super Bee to stop. It was like a bazooka: aim and pull the trigger.

Base engine: 440 cubic inches, 390 horsepower, 490 lbs-ft of torque
Base price: $4,300.00
Curb weight: 4,100 lbs
Production numbers: 1,907

1969 DODGE SUPER BEE

Chapter 16

1969 FORD MUSTANG GT 428 SCJ

In the category of "competing against yourself," Ford pulled a doozy in 1969. This is the year that the Mach 1 was released, and Ford cranked up the marketing machine to push the new model. Yet in the same stable was the Mustang GT, a nameplate that had been around since the April 1964 release of the original Mustang. Comparing the equipment levels of the 1969 GT and the new Mach 1 revealed near-identical vehicles. The Mach 1 had some visual flash that the GT didn't enjoy, but in the areas that really mattered, they were confusingly similar.

The buying public, sometimes easily confused, gravitated toward the heavily marketed and flashier Mach 1, relegating the Mustang GT to the shadows. Unlike the fastback Mach 1, the GT was offered on coupe, convertible, and SportsRoof bodies. Fortunately for the people who chose the subdued GT, the full slate of ground-shaking engines was available, including the feared 428-cubic-inchers. Two flavors of Cobra Jet engines were on the menu, the "standard" CJ mill rated at 335 horsepower and the Super Cobra Jet (SCJ), also advertised at 335 ponies.

Ford targeted the SCJ to buyers who tended to turn over the odometer a quarter-mile at a time. This package was full of race-developed components, such as a hardened cast crankshaft, 427 "Le Mans–type" capscrew connecting rods, functional Shaker hood Ram Air induction, a 31-spline Traction-Lok rear end, an external oil cooler, cast-aluminum pistons, and a starting rear axle ratio of 3.91:1. Air conditioning was not available on SCJ-equipped cars. This was a serious drag machine. Handling could be, well,

challenging, but SCJs were made to move in one direction, quickly. How fast, you ask? How about lunging down the quarter-mile in 13.9 seconds at 103 miles per hour? That makes for a very competitive package.

Base engine: 428-cubic-inch V-8, 335 horsepower, 440 lbs-ft of torque

Horsepower and torque for this car: 335 horsepower, 440 lbs-ft of torque

Base price: $2,618.00

Price of SCJ engine option: $420.96

Curb weight: 3,600 lbs

Production numbers: 5,396

1969 FORD MUSTANG GT 428 SCJ

Chapter 17

1969 SHELBY GT500 CONVERTIBLE

What had started as a way to transform a secretary's car into something that could hold its own on the road and the track had, by 1969, become a grand touring car that was a Ford Motor Company product. Though it wore "Shelby" lettering, it was no longer a product of Carroll Shelby's fertile mind. But as a grand touring car, it had few equals.

Ford introduced a new generation of Mustang in 1969, and since Shelby had been using the original pony car as the basis for its GT350s and GT500s, it was inevitable that the latest Shelby road car was going to use the newest 'Stang as a starting point. Except by 1969, the Shelby program was completely in the hands of Ford. The Blue Oval didn't want to make road-legal race cars; it wanted to build road cars that looked like they could race. The results were the GT350 and GT500, available in SportsRoof and convertible models. With extended front fenders, five functional hood scoops, and a plethora of stripes and spoilers, they were not the ideal cars for the retiring wallflower. In GT500 guise, the car packed a 428-cubic-inch Cobra Jet engine, a torque monster that didn't need high rpm to fling its host vehicle down the road. It was the perfect powerplant for the GT500, which could use the torque to smoke the rear tires at will but would be equally happy cruising up the coast for a relaxing weekend getaway.

The GT500 only needed 6 seconds to reach 60 miles per hour, but after that, it tended to run out of breath. Getting to the finish line at a drag strip required 17 seconds, not quite the same numbers that Shelbys were generating a handful of years prior. But with the top down, an aggressive rumble flowing from the center-mounted exhaust tips, and the long hood looking like it could touch the horizon, the 1969 Shelby GT500 dished up plenty of sporty style with real-world livability.

Base engine: 428-cubic-inch V-8, 335 horsepower, 440 lbs-ft of torque

Base price: $5,027.00

Curb weight: 4,230 lbs

Production numbers: 1,871

Production number for this model: 335

1969 SHELBY GT500 CONVERTIBLE

Chapter 18

1969 TORINO TALLADEGA

It's been said that racing improves the breed, and the 1969 Torino Talladega is proof that the slogan is more than a string of words. In the late 1960s, Ford was locked in a bitter battle with Dodge in NASCAR racing, but Ford's design shapes weren't in agreement with the aerodynamic dictates of NASCAR's high-speed tracks. While recessed grilles were a key component of contemporary designs, the wind tunnel showed that they were a major drag. So Ford pushed the grille on the Torino forward by six inches by extending the front fenders and mounted the headlights and grille opening flush with the front bumper. The corners were radiused to help reduce air resistance, and the front bumper was actually a reshaped rear bumper. The Torino had a fastback profile that worked well in a racing environment, and with a Gurney flap on the tail, aerodynamic drag was reduced. The rocker panels were rolled under the car, increasing ground clearance by an inch. Then the front end on the race car would be lowered, giving the vehicle effective downforce at speed. Ford named the vehicle after the racetrack where the race car would be seeing its highest speeds: Talladega.

NASCAR regulations required that a manufacturer sell at least 500 street-legal examples to the public, and Ford met that rule and more. A total of 754 were built at Ford's Atlanta, Georgia, plant. The only option on the cars was the choice of colors: Wimbledon White, Presidential Blue, or Royal Maroon. While the very successful race versions packed Boss 429 engines, the street cars used the stout 428 Cobra Jet, a far cheaper engine to assemble than the Boss 429. Rated at 335 horsepower, the Cobra Jet could muscle the street Talladega to a 130-mile-per-hour top speed. With 440 lb-ft of torque, 60 miles per hour came up on the speedometer in just 5.8 seconds. Yes, racing can improve the breed.

Base engine: 428-cubic-inch V-8, 335 horsepower, 440 lbs-ft of torque
Base price: $3,570
Curb weight: 3,775
Production numbers: 754

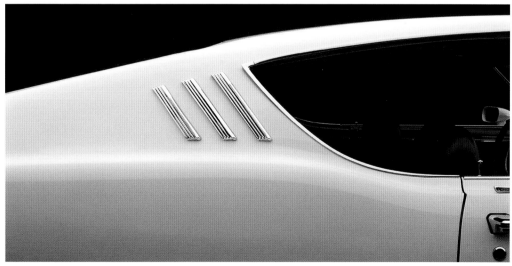

1969 TORINO TALLADEGA

Chapter 19

1969 MERCURY CYCLONE SPOILER CALE YARBOROUGH SPECIAL

As the 1960s were drawing to a close, Mercury was competing heavily in NASCAR, a venue that was seeing aerodynamics play an increasingly important role in vehicle performance. It soon became clear that the front end of the division's Cyclone generated far too much drag to put it at the front of the pack.

The fix came in the form of a lengthened front end. Cyclone Spoilers were shipped to Holman-Moody, where the front end was sliced off and an extension was welded on. With a front end that extended almost 20 inches over stock, the result was known as the Cyclone Spoiler. The lengthened nose, in conjunction with a flush grille and headlight assembly, clove the air like a big knife. The race cars became highly competitive, and they won a fair share of races.

But in order to roll a race car onto the grid, NASCAR required any manufacturer to make at least 500 street-legal examples available to the public. To honor Mercury stock car driver Cale Yarborough, Mercury released a commemorative edition, replete with a red-and-white paint scheme, Yarborough's colors.

Fitted with a 351-cubic-inch Windsor V-8 rated at 290 horsepower, and attached to an automatic transmission, the eye-catching fastback retailed for $3,800, and could cover the quarter-mile in 15.6 seconds at 94 miles per hour. This example is one of only 41 fitted with the optional 428 Cobra Jet engine, rated at 335 horsepower and 385 lb-ft of torque. Few muscle cars have ever been as closely tied to the competition arena as the Cyclone Spoiler.

Base engine: 351-cubic-inch V-8, 290 horsepower, 385 lbs-ft of torque

Base price: $3,800

Curb weight: 3,580 lbs

Production numbers: 519

1969 MERCURY CYCLONE SPOILER II

Chapter 20

1969 MERCURY CYCLONE SPOILER DAN GURNEY EDITION

It's hard to believe, but there was a time when stock cars actually raced in stock cars racing. American auto manufacturers were in the thick of battle on NASCAR tracks from coast to coast, taking advantage of the "win on Sunday, sell on Monday" marketing. Ford was in the middle of the fray, and in order to expose the public to cars from the Blue Oval family, it was decided in Dearborn that the upscale Mercury brand would race for its dinner.

The vehicle that rolled onto both NASCAR and road-racing starting grids was the Cyclone Spoiler II, a Mercury version of the fastback Ford Torino. Racing success came to Mercury, and to commemorate road-racing great Dan Gurney's victories in 1968, Mercury released a road-car edition for 1969. Clad in Gurney's traditional blue-and-white racing colors, the Dan Gurney Edition Cyclone Spoiler II used a Ford Windsor 351-cubic-inch V-8 that checked in with 290 horsepower. All 218 built used the column-shift FMX automatic transmission. Options were nonexistent; the Dan Gurney Edition was a complete package, though a few were built with the heater deleted. At the rear a tail spoiler lifted from the Mustang added some downforce; the cars were shipped to the dealer with the wing in the trunk, and it was installed during the vehicle prep process.

Handling was period correct, which means it was somewhat ponderous. A front anti-sway bar, stiff springs, and a solid rear axle contributed to a driving experience best described as "classic muscle car," meaning that it was comfortable in a straight line, but everything else was something of a challenge. But like most muscle cars, the Dan Gurney Edition performed its intended straight-line duties with brutal efficiency.

Base engine: 351-cubic-inch V-8, 290 horsepower, 385 lbs-ft of torque

Base price: $3,800

Curb weight: 3,580 lbs

Production numbers: 519

1969 MERCURY CYCLONE SPOILER

Chapter 21

1970 AMC AMX

Few people would use "muscle car" and "American Motors" in the same sentence, but in fact, AMC put a toe in the performance waters with surprisingly impressive results. With a lineup of staid vehicles like the Rambler and Ambassador, performance enthusiasts were surprised when the Marlin debuted in 1967, followed the next year by the AMX. Developed as a response to the Mustang, it was a true two-seater, bereft of a rear seat. Riding on a relatively short 97-inch wheelbase, it debuted with a range of engines, from a 225-horsepower, 290-cubic-inch V-8 to the beefy 315-horsepower, 390-cubic-inch powerplant. Combined with the vehicle's light weight (3,205 lbs), the stout engine could propel the AMX to 60 miles per hour in just 6.6 seconds. But sales were less than stellar, with only 8,293 sold.

American Motors had high hopes for the refreshed 1970 version. With its increasingly aggressive styling, AMC hoped that the AMX would appeal to both muscle car and sports car enthusiasts, two camps that rarely acknowledged each other's existences. AMC marketed it as "the only American sports car under $4,000," which was not the best way to grab the attention of a muscle car driver. The base 360-cubic-inch engine now cranked out 290 ponies, while the tire-melting 390 engine was rated at 325 horsepower. With the big engine, the AMX could cover the quarter-mile in 14.68 seconds at 92 miles per hour, about the same as many of its competitors. The only problem was the 1970 AMX, a quick car that handled like a sports car, confused the buying public. Most muscle car

enthusiasts only wanted a fast-in-a-straight-line machine and couldn't care less about going around a corner. On the sports car side, the market really didn't warm up to the capable canyon carver. In trying to make the AMX all things to the enthusiast market, AMC watered down the message. Sales of the two-seater suffered, with only 4,116 sold. American Motors released a four-seater for 1971, chasing better sales. But that's another story . . .

Base engine: 360-cubic-inch V-8, 290 horsepower, 395 lbs-ft of torque

Optional engine: 390-cubic-inch V-8, 325 horsepower, 420 lbs-ft of torque

Base price: $3,395

Curb weight: 3,126 lbs

Production numbers: 4,116

Chapter 22

1970 BUICK GRAN SPORT GSX

Buick had a reputation as a builder of solid but ho-hum vehicles up until the 1960s. This is when *performance*, long a dirty word at Buick, started creeping into the division's vernacular. Vehicles like the Riviera, a boulevard cruiser, became, in Gran Sport guise, potent performers. The midsize Skylark responded especially well to the GS treatment, and as the '60s drew to a close, Buick steadily fed the public's appetite for luxurious muscle.

A refreshed body design for the Skylark debuted in 1970, and Buick wasted no time in creating a Gran Sport version. Yet that wasn't enough for this division, which was by now mad with power; they released an even hotter version of a hot car, the GSX. General Motors had invested heavily in making the 112-inch-wheelbase A-body platform a repository for massive cubic inches, and Buick's version didn't scrimp on the power. Equipped with a 455-cubic-inch V-8 rated at 315 horsepower in base form, the big mill cranked out a tire-churning 345 horses in Stage 1 form. Both engines generated torque figures that a locomotive would envy, 510 lbs-ft, to be exact. Only two colors were offered, Apollo White and Saturn Yellow. These high-visibility vehicles didn't sell in huge numbers—Buick built just 678 of them in 1970—but they were halo cars, able to go head to head with the Chevelle LS6, the GTO Judge, and the Oldsmobile 4-4-2 W-30. Only 199 were equipped with manual transmissions, but regardless of how the gears

were changed, the vivid Buick could haul its 3,874 lbs to 60 miles per hour in only 5.80 seconds, which is remarkable when you factor in the tires of the era. With its functional hood scoops feeding air to the 750cfm Quadra-Jet four-barrel, it could cover the quarter-mile in 13.38 seconds at 105.5 mph. Those are impressive numbers for any muscle car, especially a Buick. For a brief time, the "doctor's division" was running in the fast lane, figuratively and literally.

Base engine: 455-cubic-inch V-8, 360 horsepower, 510 lbs-ft of torque

Base price: $4,880

Curb weight: 4,000 lbs

Production numbers: 687

1970 BUICK GRAN SPORT GSX

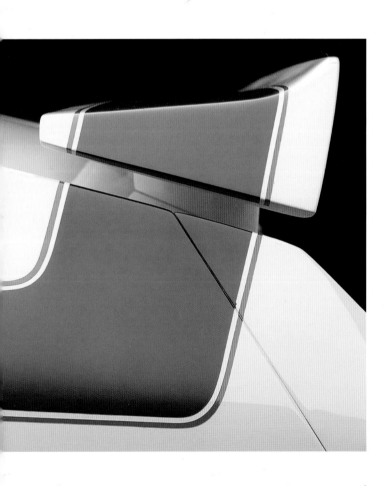

Chapter 23

1970 1/2 CHEVROLET CAMARO Z28 RS

Since its introduction in 1967, the Camaro had received just a mild restyle for 1969. But when the 1970 model was rolled out halfway through the 1970 model year (which is why this car is usually called a 1970 1/2 model), it was clearly a step in a different direction. With its European influences, the newest Camaro was slippery and sleek, the repository of considerable horsepower. Unlike most of the muscle cars on the market, the Z28 possessed a trait that few of its competitors could emulate: the ability to turn and stop like a sports car. Chevrolet had built the best of all worlds.

With the relaxing of the SCCA's engine displacement regulations, Chevy was able to increase the Z28's engine displacement. Now boasting 350 cubes, it possessed impressive low-end torque, so necessary on the street. Yet with a crankcase full of race-honed components, the Corvette-sourced, LT1, solid-filter engine would spin to its redline like a top. With 11.0:1 compression, four-bolt main bearing caps, forged crankshaft, aggressive camshaft, and topped by a huge 780cfm No. 4150 Holley four-barrel carburetor, the 1970 1/2 Z28 proved that Chevrolet still took performance seriously.

Like the Z28s before it, the 1970 1/2 version was adept at handling a curve. Thanks to advances in suspension and tire technology, the new Z28's handling was nothing short of amazing. Many muscle cars had more horsepower than the Z/28, but few could put it down to the ground as efficiently.

Like the ad says, power is nothing without control. The 1970 1/2 Z28 could have been the poster car for control. Yet it delivered speed when the whip was put down. Sixty miles per hour was reached in only 6.1 seconds, and the quarter-mile could be covered in 14.4 seconds at 99.1 miles per hour.

Base engine: 350-cubic-inch V-8, 360 horsepower, 380 lbs-ft of torque

Base price: $3,412.00

Price of Z28 option: $573.00

Curb weight: 3,850 lbs

Production numbers: 8,733

1970 1/2 CHEVROLET CAMARO Z28 RS

1970 1/2 CHEVROLET CAMARO Z28 RS

Chapter 24

1970 CHEVELLE SS 454 LS6

At the end of any performance enthusiast's day, bench racing in the garage while drinking a beer, most arguments tend to come to a close when someone drops the name Chevelle LS6 into the mix. Even among muscle car crazies, the Chevelle LS6 was the automotive perfect storm—a heady combination of broad-shoulder styling and brutal power. Its 454-cubic-inch V-8, rated at 450 horsepower and 500 lbs-ft of torque, generated all that and more. Vaulting to 60 miles per hour in only 5.4 seconds takes staggering amounts of grunt, especially in a street-legal vehicle. With its über-heavy-duty internal components, 11.25:1 compression ratio, and solid-lifter camshaft, the $263.30 LS6 option had more in common with pure race cars than the car next door. How many automatic transmission–equipped grocery-getters could haul down the drag strip in 13.81 seconds at 103.8 miles per hour? Thought so.

Under the aggressive bodywork lurked the vaunted F41 suspension, with stiffer springs installed to handle the iron block's considerable weight. Functional cowl induction helped the big-block to ingest cool air, while a 2½-inch exhaust system created a memorable soundtrack. The vast majority of LS6 engines were installed in Chevelles, with a small number finding their way into El Caminos. Chevrolet outfitted 4,475 vehicles with the LS6, creating an instant classic. Even in 1970, performance enthusiasts knew the option was something special. It would become the performance benchmark, not only for General Motors, but for its competition. This was an era when bigger was definitely better. Chrysler had the 426 Hemi, Ford had the Boss 429, and Chevrolet had the 454 LS6. You don't want to show up at a gun fight with a knife; you want to show up with a shotgun. This was a shotgun.

Base engine: 454-cubic-inch V-8, 450 horsepower, 500 lbs-ft of torque

Base price: $3,800

Price of LS6 engine option: $766

Curb weight: 3,800 lbs

Production numbers: 8,773—total SS 454

Number produced with this engine: 4,475

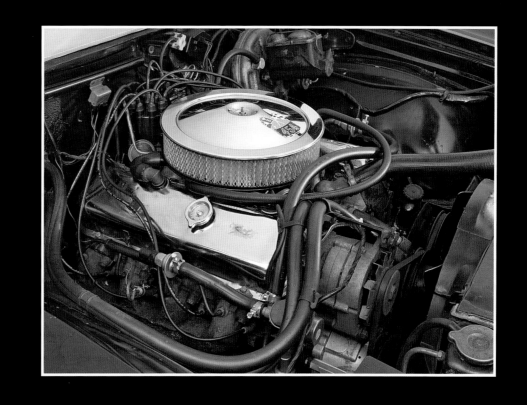

Chapter 25

1970 DODGE CHALLENGER R/T CONVERTIBLE

Most muscle cars were closed conveyances, usually coupes, but sometimes posts. But a fair number were convertibles, and with a sufficiently robust engine, a ragtop could more than hold its own with its peers. And in the Challenger RT, even the base engine was more than strong enough to gain the car's entry into the fraternity of muscle cars. In the auto magazines, it seems like every performance car is equipped with a huge, expensive engine, ready to transform the rear tires into clouds of smoke at any opportunity. In reality, the vast majority of performance-car buyers tended to buy vehicles with more insurance-friendly powerplants. Challenger customers were no different, and the capable 383-cubic-inch V-8 was a flexible, strong engine that didn't cost a king's ransom to buy or keep in gasoline. Rated at 335 horsepower, it rode in a 110-inch-wheelbase platform, 2 inches longer than its Plymouth 'Cuda sibling.

Chrysler introduced the E-body, a car designed in the pony car mold, for the 1970 model year. It had taken Chrysler Corporation seven years after the debut of the Mustang to get a direct competitor on the street, but when Dodge finally unleashed its entry into the pony car market, it was a winner. This was an era when Chrysler was known for its engineering

creativity, and the Challenger enjoyed the fruits of that knowledge. Boasting a torsion bar front suspension and a wide range of powerplants, the Challenger was targeted at buyers who leaned a bit more toward comfort than 'Cuda customers. Designed by Carl Cameron, the Challenger hewed to the classic pony car formula of long hood and short deck proportions, yet it could be equipped with a bevy of engines, including the 426 Hemi. In that guise, the Challenger was a straight-line beast. But in the real world, performance enthusiasts who wanted to work on their suntans while affording their fun didn't have to look any further than a Challenger 383 convertible.

Base engine: 383-cubic-inch V-8, 335 horsepower, 425 lbs-ft of torque
Optional engines: 440-cubic-inch V-8, 1x4 barrel, 375 horsepower, 425 lb-ft of torque; 440-cubic-inch V-8, 3x2-barrel, 390 horsepower, 480 lb-ft of torque; 426-cubic-inch V-8, 425 horsepower, 490 lbs-ft of torque
Base price: $3,535
Curb weight: 3,525 lbs
Production numbers: 3,979

1970 DODGE CHALLENGER R/T CONVERTIBLE

Chapter 26

1970 DODGE CHALLENGER T/A

When the Pentastar group introduced the new E-body pony cars for the 1970 model year, it sought new racing venues in which to promote its sporty new offerings. With the Sports Car Club of America's Trans-Am Sedan Champion racing series finding favor with the buying public, Chrysler Corporation saw an opportunity to promote its new Challengers and 'Cudas in the ultra-competitive series.

In order for a manufacturer to compete, it had to put a minimum number of like vehicles on the street. And in order to field a Sam Posey–driven Challenger T/A (T/A obviously standing for "Trans-Am," the series in which it raced) on the starting grid, Dodge assembled 2,142 street-going units, more than enough to satisfy the SCCA's homologation requirements. While SCCA rules limited the race engine's displacement to 305 cubic inches, for 1970 road-going versions no longer had to comply with that displacement limit. The race team met the displacement regulation by de-stroking a 340-cubic-inch engine to 303.8 cubic inches, but the street version retained its 340-cubic-inch displacement, advertising that fact with large decals on the side of the vehicle.

Another deviation from the competition car was the production auto's use of multiple carburetors. Posey's race car breathed through a single four-barrel carburetor, but the street cars used a "Six-Pak" induction system consisting of three two-barrel carbs. Beneath the intake manifold, the factory performed a number of performance tweaks, including stress-relieving the iron block and ensuring that the main bearing cap area had plenty of room for the installation of four-bolt caps. The Challenger T/A was rated at 290 horsepower, suspiciously similar to Ford's and GM's Trans-Am street cars. Dodge stated that peak power came on at 5,000 rpm, yet the engine's redline was a lofty 6,500. The quarter-mile could be run in 14.5 seconds, crossing the line at a tick over 100 miles per hour.

With the growing resistance by the insurance companies to cover muscle cars in the early 1970s, performance was starting to become a tough sell. Dodge hoped to sell a Challenger T/A in 1971, going so far as to photograph a mock-up for advertising. But the decision makers stepped away from that idea, making the 1970 Challenger T/A a one-year-only model.

Base engine: 340-cubic-inch V-8, 3x2 barrel, 290 horsepower, 345 lbs-ft of torque
Base price: $4,480
Curb weight: 3,650
Production numbers: 2,539

1970 DODGE CHALLENGER T/A

Chapter 27

1970 DODGE CHARGER R/T 440-6

In the classic sense, a muscle car is a relatively inexpensive midsize car with a huge engine, aimed at the young and young-at-heart who want to generate insane speeds in an affordable package. The 1970 Charger fit the bill perfectly. The base six-cylinder Charger listed for just $3,711; even by moving to the top-shelf R/T model, a buyer still only had to shell out $3,711. Of course, for customers with a penchant for laying waste to rear tires, Dodge would install the healthy 440 Six-Pak engine, rated at 390 horsepower, or the famed 426 Hemi, generating 425 horsepower.

Since anyone could enter a showroom and drive off in a muscular car, some customers wanted a vehicle that stood out from the crowd. In 1970, no car company could touch Chrysler for making colors available that, in bright sunlight, could threaten your retinas. One of the most vivid was Panther Pink, paint code FM3. Covering a muscle car in such a hue was like seeing a Folies Bergère show—at first glance it was shocking, then it tended to grow on you.

With 9,370 units sold, sales of the 1970 Charger R/T reflected the public's growing disinterest in performance cars. Chrysler stole some of the Charger R/T's thunder by releasing the new E-body coupes in 1970, contributing to the Charger's diminishing sales. Insurance companies were starting to demand that auto manufacturers build more "socially responsible" vehicles and began raising the premiums on performance models. This had a cooling effect on muscle car sales. But for the enthusiast, there would always be a need for a car like the Charger.

Base engine: 440-cubic-inch V-8, 375 horsepower, 480 lbs-ft of torque

Optional engines: 440-cubic-inch V-8, 3x2-barrel carbs, 390 horsepower, 490 lbs-ft of torque; 426-cubic-inch V-8, 425 horsepower, 490 lbs-ft of torque

Base price: $3,711.00

Curb weight: 3,638 lbs

Production numbers: 10,337

Number produced with this engine: 116

1970 DODGE CHARGER R/T 440-6

Chapter 28

1970 FORD MUSTANG BOSS 302

Ford's Mustang walked a fine line between pony car, sports car, and muscle car. Depending on the engine, it could fall into any one category. Or, like the Boss 302, it could cover all three. Built to satisfy the SCCA's requirements for a Trans-Am race car in 1969, the Boss 302 would go head to head with the Chevrolet Camaro Z/28 and Pontiac Trans Am. The hotly contested series continued into 1970, with Chrysler entering the fray with its E-bodies. Regulations kept engine displacement below 5 liters, and Ford installed a 302-cubic-inch engine in both the race and street versions. The solid-lifter engine of the road cars was factory-rated at 290 horsepower, a laughably low figure. In reality, it was churning out on the order of 350 ponies, and high-rpm ones at that.

Being designed for road racing, the Boss 302 featured substantial underpinnings, including front disc brakes, a large front roll bar, beefed-up shock towers, and strengthened front spindles. Buyers could get any transmission they wanted, as long as they wanted a close-ratio four-speed manual. With its huge valves set in Cleveland heads, the '70 Boss 302 engine needed fuel, and lots of it. Perched atop the powerplant was a huge 780cfm Holley carburetor, helping to generate rotational energy that could haul the Boss 302 down the drag strip in 14.93 seconds at 93.45 miles per hour. That's serious muscle car performance. That it could corner like a slot car was frosting on the cake.

Famed designer Larry Shinoda penned the Boss 302's exterior, including the dramatic graphics package. Base price of a Boss 302 was $3,720, and it was money well spent. Ford built 7,013 Boss 302s in 1970, a significant improvement over the 1,628 made the year before. The year 1970 would be the Boss 302's final year; in 1971 it was replaced with the Boss 351, since racing regulations for 1971 no longer required set engine displacements. But for two years, Ford's Tran-Am racer was a multi-category crowd pleaser.

Base engine: 302-cubic-inch V-8, 290 horsepower, 290 lbs-ft of torque
Base price: $3,720
Curb weight: 3,300
Production numbers: 7.013

1970 FORD MUSTANG BOSS 302

Chapter 29

1970 FORD MUSTANG BOSS 429

Ford knew that winning in NASCAR meant building an engine capable of beating Chrysler's mighty 426 Hemi. Because the Hemi engine was kicking everyone's butts, Ford developed semi-hemispherical heads for its engine.

Regulations required that Ford install at least 500 engines in street cars. This seemed like an ideal opportunity to build the Mustang into a killer muscle car. Ford tasked its race shop, Kar Kraft, with turning fastback Mustangs into Boss 429s. The Brighton, Michigan, firm shoehorned the 429-cubic-inch race engine into a 1969 Mustang and called it a Boss 429. They rated it at 375 horsepower.

On paper, Ford had the ultimate muscle car. Unfortunately, most cars live on the street and not on sheets of paper, and in the real world the Boss 429 didn't run like the competition. In an effort to make the cantankerous engine streetable, Ford bolted on a 735cfm Holley carburetor and a set of cast-iron exhaust manifolds. Big race engines don't like little carburetors and restrictive exhaust manifolds. The result was less than stellar. One period magazine, *Car Life*, hammered a stock 1969 Boss 429 down the drag strip in 14.09 seconds at 102.85 miles per hour. Nice numbers, but not enough to keep a 426 Hemi driver awake at night. But the clever lads at *Car Life* installed a set of headers and a larger carburetor and then hurled the car down the quarter-mile again. This time they posted a time of 12.32 seconds at 113.49 miles per hour. That was more like it! Ford found good homes for only 847 Boss 429s in 1969; muscle car enthusiasts had gotten the word that this expensive model ($1,208.35 for the engine alone) was something of a dog out of the box. Granted, with a little work, an owner could uncork a monster of an engine, but most buyers wanted to kick butt right off the showroom floor.

The Boss 429 was a model of visual modesty. The discreet decals on the lower front fenders and the functional hood scoop large enough to ingest a small pet were the only exterior indications that this wasn't your pedestrian Mustang fastback.

In 1970, the Boss 429 was still on the order form, even though Ford had essentially pulled out of racing, thus eliminating the need to build a street car with a race-car engine. Marketing the beast slipped even lower on Ford's list of things to do in 1970; thus, the Boss 429 sold in small numbers—499 to be exact. The bottom line was suffering with every Boss 429 Ford built, so they pulled the plug at the end of the 1970 model year, and Ford's most serious attempt at a muscle car was consigned to the history books.

Base engine: 429-cubic inch V-8, 375 horsepower, 450 lbs-ft of torque
Base price: $2,771
Price of Boss 429 option: $1,208
Curb weight: 3,870 lbs
Production numbers: 499

1970 FORD MUSTANG BOSS 429

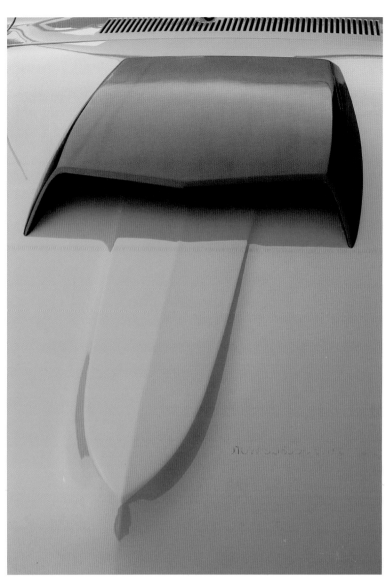

1970 FORD MUSTANG BOSS 429

Chapter 30

1970 OLDSMOBILE 4-4-2 W-30 CONVERTIBLE

A doctor's car. For decades, that's the image that Oldsmobile carefully nurtured. Firmly located in the middle of the divisional stepladder, Olds took care to build solid, well-crafted road cars, possessing adequate performance and very comfortable appointments.

That equation was knocked askew in the 1960s; Oldsmobile was not immune to the rising influence of the performance-loving baby-boom generation. The 4-4-2 debuted in the 1964 model year as a gentleman's muscle car. As the decade wore on, the 4-4-2 retained that focus on luxury, but with each new year came new power. When the 1970 edition rolled into showrooms, the 4-4-2, especially in W-30 trim, was one of the most civilized muscle cars on the market. It was also one of the most powerful.

The W-30 option was a performance enthusiast's dream, complete with functional forced air induction, plastic inner fender liners, a fiberglass hood, and an aluminum intake manifold. What matters in muscle car land are quarter-mile results, and with a time of 14.2 seconds at 102 miles per hour, the 4-4-2 W-30 delivered quarter-mile results.

Unlike many of its muscle car contemporaries, the 4-4-2 could find its way around a corner without embarrassing itself. Oldsmobile engineers did a commendable job tuning the suspension to deliver a comfortable ride while effectively putting the power to the pavement. Of course, if a driver wished to generate clouds of tire smoke, the 4-4-2 could make that happen with little effort, thanks to 500 lbs-ft of torque.

Base engine: 455-cubic-inch V-8, 365 horsepower, 500 lbs-ft of torque
Horsepower and torque for optional engine: 370 horsepower, 500 lbs-ft of torque
Base price: $3,567.00
Curb weight: 3,740 lbs
Production numbers: 2,933
Production of this model: 264

1970 OLDSMOBILE 4-4-2 W-30 CONVERTIBLE

Chapter 31

1970 PLYMOUTH 'CUDA CONVERTIBLE 440

It took a while, but Chrysler finally released a proper pony car some five years after Ford invented the genre (the original A-body Barracuda was more of a small sedan than a pony car). The new E-body came in two iterations: the Plymouth Barracuda and the Dodge Challenger. Chrysler positioned Plymouth as an entry-level, value-rich nameplate, on a par with General Motors' Chevrolet. When the Barracuda hit the market, it was targeted at buyers who wanted a dash of sport, a dash of style, and a bucketful of performance. Plymouth's E-body came in three flavors: the Barracuda, the Gran Coupe, and the muscular 'Cuda.

The 'Cuda came standard with a 383-cubic-inch V-8, rated at 335 horsepower. Optional engines included the 440-6 and the 426 Hemi, but this 'Cuda features the user-friendly 440-cubic-inch Magnum engine topped with a single Carter four-barrel, a $249.55 option that generated 375 horsepower. It would cover the quarter-mile in the 14-second range. Two transmissions were available, an A-833 four-speed manual and a 727 Torqueflite three-speed automatic. Regardless of which gearbox handled the engine's prodigious output, care had to be exercised on anything but bone-dry roads. 'Cuda buyers wanting neck-snapping performance with a side of fresh air sprang for the convertible, which started at $3,433. Only 635 ragtop 'Cudas were built.

Chrysler came late to the pony-car arena, yet it built one of the most stunning muscle cars on the road. Instead of trying to do all things well, it sacrificed characteristics like good handling and braking in return for exceptional competence at generating whiplash. Most importantly, it looked good while doing it. Isn't that the purpose of muscle cars?

Base engine: 383-cubic-inch V-8, 335 horsepower, 425 lbs-ft of torque

Optional engines: 340-cubic-inch V-8, 275 horsepower, 340 lbs-ft of torque;
440-cubic-inch V-8, 375 horsepower, 480 lbs-ft of torque;
440-cubic-inch V-8, 3x2-barrel carbs, 390 horsepower, 490 lbs-ft of torque;
426-cubic-inch V-8, 425 horsepower, 490 lbs-ft of torque

Base price: $3,164.00

Price of engine option: $249.55

Curb weight: 3,555 lbs

Production numbers: 18,880 coupes; 635 convertibles

Number produced with this engine: 28

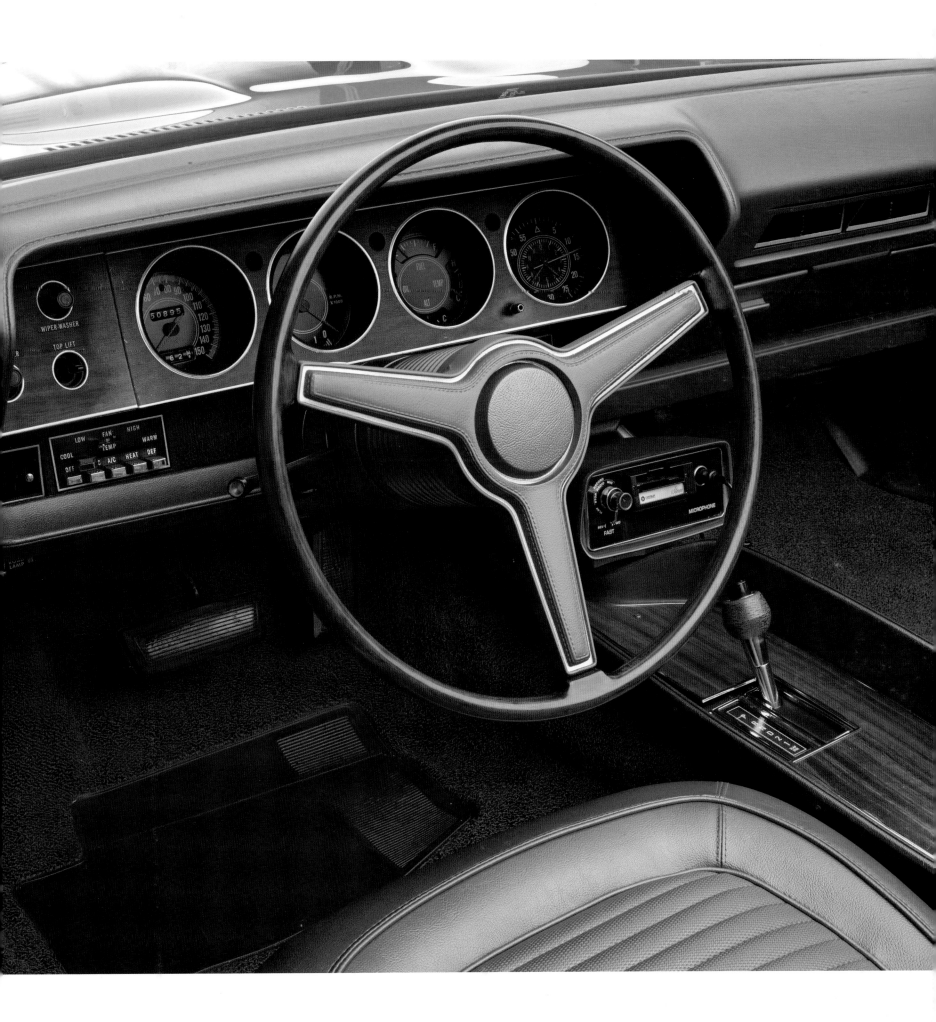

1970 PLYMOUTH 'CUDA CONVERTIBLE 440

Chapter 32

1970 PLYMOUTH AAR 'CUDA

Most muscle cars were intended for one purpose: to go in a straight line as fast as possible, preferably in quarter-mile increments. But a select few muscle cars were designed to handle twists and turns with aplomb. These were the vehicles intended for use in the SCCA's Trans-Am racing series. Before a car could show up on the race grid, it had to show up in dealers' showrooms. Plymouth, in the thick of competition, wanted to benefit from the glory of professional racing, especially since Chevrolet had won two Trans-Am titles. But to go racing, Plymouth needed to build a car that the public could buy.

Enter the AAR 'Cuda. Plymouth signed up famed racer Dan Gurney to lead its attack in the Trans-Am series, and his team, All American Racers (AAR) put a viable race car on the track. Plymouth, in turn, put a street-legal version into customers' hands. Equipped with the flexible 340-cubic-inch engine, the AAR 'Cuda looked every inch a race car. Atop the engine was a Six-Pak carburetion setup with three two-barrel carbs feeding the hungry engine. The fiberglass hood had a huge NACA duct guiding air into the induction system, while at the other end of the engine, chromed exhaust tips peeked out from beneath the body in front of the rear tires. Unlike many muscle cars, the AAR could carve a corner with the best Detroit had to offer. With its Z/28, Chevrolet had shown that a market existed for a strong vehicle that could do more than accelerate like a banshee.

Plymouth copied the race-car paint scheme to give the street car visual pizzazz. With a full-length strobe stripe, front and rear spoilers, and Gurney's AAR logo on the rear fender, the E-body was tough to overlook. And the fast-looking car was fast; 0–60 came in 5.8 seconds, and the quarter-mile was dispatched in 14.4 seconds at 99.5 miles per hour, fast enough to run with any of its big-block competition.

Base engine: 340-cubic-inch V-8, 290 horsepower, 345 lbs-ft of torque
Base price: $4,340.00
Curb weight: 3,600 lbs
Production numbers: 2,724

Chapter 33

1970 PLYMOUTH ROAD RUNNER

It's hard to imagine an automobile being named after a cartoon character today. Calling a car a "Sponge Bob" or a "Square Pants" would be a term of derision. This has long been the case (a certain mouse from Burbank comes to mind). Yet Plymouth took a bare-boned, broad-shouldered B-body muscle car and graced it with the name "Road Runner," which was a popular Warner Brothers cartoon character at the time (Chrysler paid Warner Bros. a royalty for the use of the name).

The Road Runner may have looked like a huge bar of soap on wheels, but the result of combining a stripped-down street racer and a cartoon character was pure muscle car: a big engine in a midsize platform, designed to go arrow-straight and not cost a lot of money. At $2,896, the Road Runner coupe was within reach of any pump jockey who could scrape together a down payment. Granted, the life span of a vehicle like this was shorter than the payment book, but for a driver looking for an exhilarating ride for a modest sum, the Road Runner was hard to beat.

When equipped with a Magnum 440 engine graced with the desirable Six-Pak induction system, the Road Runner generated 390 horsepower and a massive 490 lbs-ft of torque. On the drag strip, a Road Runner 440-6 would race down to the finish line in the 14-second range, flashing through the lights at 100 miles per hour. Big-block Road Runner owners tended to become chummy with their local tire dealers.

Plymouth wasn't shy about coating their muscle cars in vibrant hues that seem to shout, "Yes, I have a fast, loud car. Give me a speeding ticket now." Colors like the Plum Crazy shown here turned heads, for better or for worse. This was not an ideal automobile for an introvert. But what would you expect from a car named after a cartoon character?

Base engine: 383-cubic-inch V-8, 335 horsepower, 425 lbs-ft of torque
Optional engines: 440-cubic-inch V-8, 375 horsepower, 480 lbs-ft of torque;
440-cubic-inch V-8, 3x2 barrel, 390 horsepower, 490 lbs-ft of torque;
426-cubic-inch V-8, 425 horsepower, 490 lbs-ft of torque
Base price: $3.034
Price of 440-6 engine option: $249.55
Curb weight: 3,475 lbs
Production numbers: 41,484

Chapter 34

1970 PLYMOUTH ROAD RUNNER SUPERBIRD

In 1969, the NASCAR aero wars were going full bore. Ford's Torino Talladega and Mercury Cyclone Spoiler II had been beating Dodge's Charger 500 on the track. Dodge retaliated with the Charger Daytona, but Plymouth felt left out in the cold. It wanted a winged car so that it, too, could be a serious player on the racetrack. Chrysler agreed, and the company unveiled the Road Runner Superbird for 1970.

With a lusty 440-cubic-inch engine and a single four-barrel carburetor, this 6,000-mile survivor had plenty of power. Optional engines included a 440-6 and the 426 Hemi. The engine choices were outrageous, but not as outrageous as the car itself; everyone's attention was drawn to the wild bodywork, designed to glue the car to the racetrack at triple-digit speeds. The Superbird didn't share any bodywork with its Daytona cousin; in fact, the hood and front fenders were sourced from the Dodge Coronet. The radical front nose and the huge rear wing were expressly Superbird components. To get the attention of the few people who weren't gawking at the bodywork, Plymouth licensed the Road Runner cartoon character to liven up the car's image. And as if the shape of the car wasn't enough, Plymouth coated the cars in outrageous colors, like the Corporation Blue and Lemon Twist examples shown here. Drivers soon found that slamming the accelerator pedal to the floor livened up the car as well, since the quarter-mile could be covered in 14.26 seconds at 103.7 miles per hour. With its slippery shape minimizing wind resistance, the Superbird could accelerate until it ran out of motor.

On the track, the Superbird lived up to Plymouth's expectations, taking the checkered flag at the 1970 Daytona 500. On the street, it didn't move off of dealers' lots with equal verve with many vehicles languishing for months before finding homes. Today they suffer no such indignity.

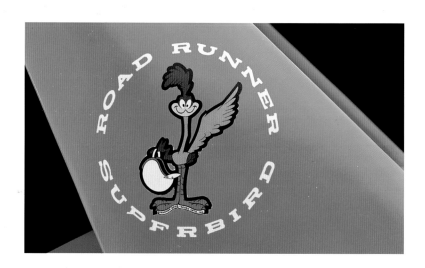

Base engine: 440-cubic-inch V-8, 375 horsepower, 480 lbs-ft of torque

Optional engines: 440-cubic-inch V-8, 3x2-barrel carbs, 390 horsepower, 490 lbs-ft of torque; 426-cubic-inch V-8, 425 horsepower, 480 lbs-ft of torque

Base price: $4,298.00

Curb weight: 3,841 lbs

Production numbers: 1,935

Number produced with this engine: 1,257

1970 PLYMOUTH ROAD RUNNER SUPERBIRD

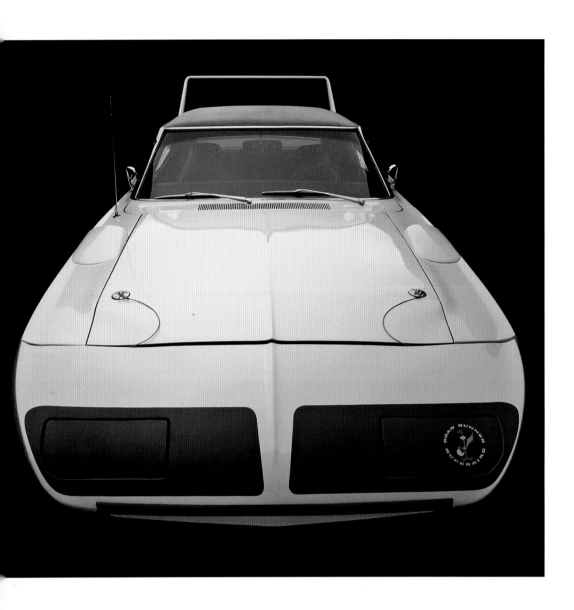

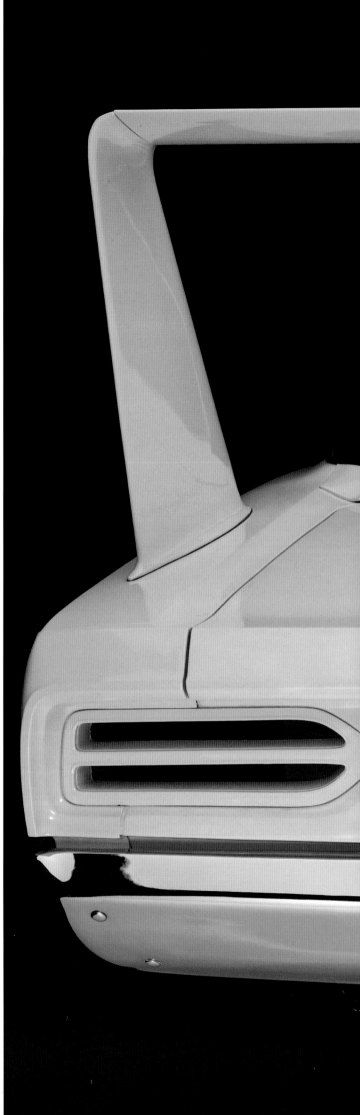

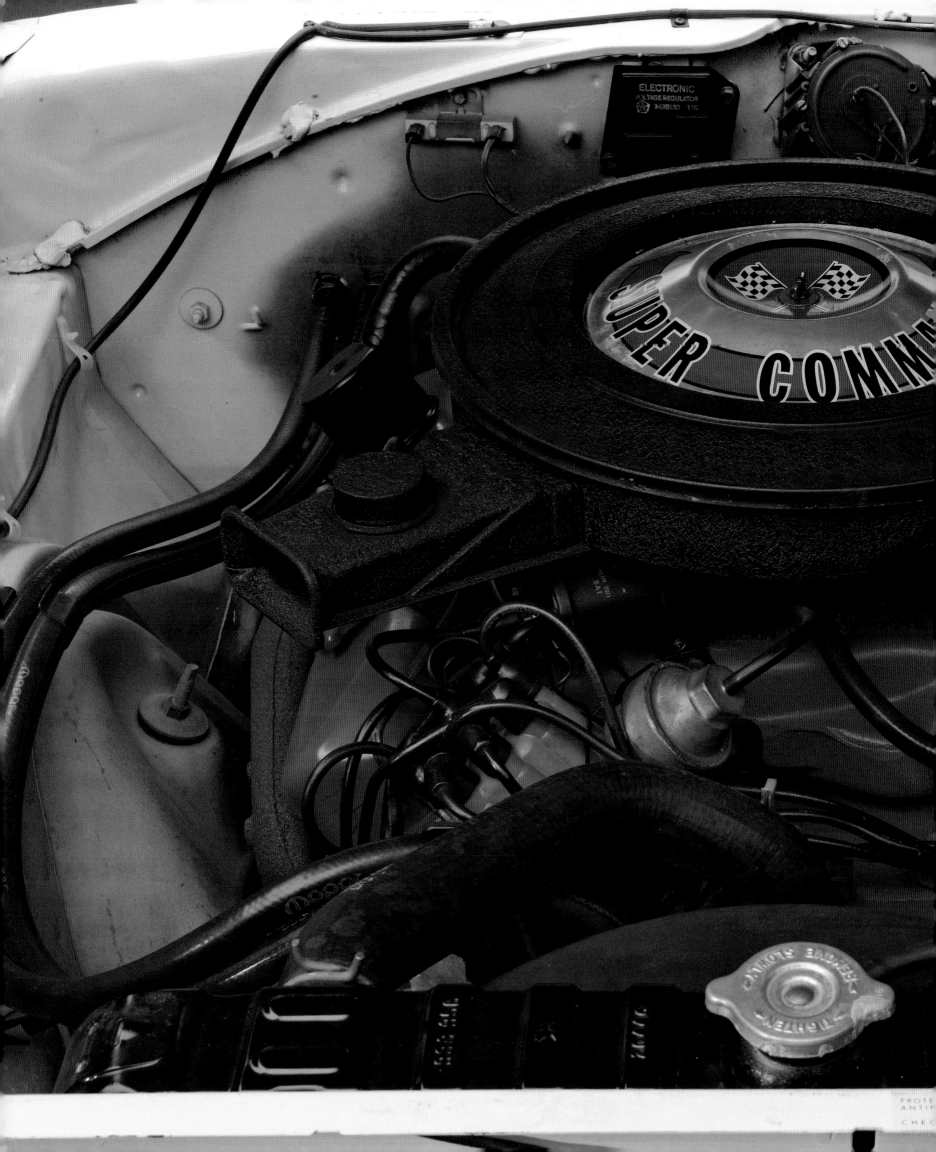

RTANT   —WARNING—
O'F WITH CHRYSLER   ALWAYS MAKE SURE COOLANT HAS
LENE GLYCOL TYPE   PROPER AMOUNT OF CHRYSLER ANTI-
DATE   FREEZE. SEE OWNER'S MANUAL FOR
ALER   COOLING SYSTEMS RECOMMENDATIONS

Chapter 35

1970 PONTIAC GTO JUDGE CONVERTIBLE RAM AIR IV

It's good to be King. Or the Judge. Pulling up to a stoplight in a GTO Judge with Ram Air IV decals on the hood pretty much resulted in groveling and muttering from surrounding drivers. The Judge's reputation on the street was such that unless you were packing some very serious metal beneath the hood, maybe an LS6 or a Hemi, your time would be spent better elsewhere. The GTO Ram Air IV was 400 cubic inches of attitude. Pontiac rated it at 370 horsepower—who says marketing types don't have a sense of humor?—and 445 lbs-ft of torque, though the real output was probably closer to 500 lbs-ft. That's stump-pulling power. This round-port-headed mill was good for at least 450 horses on demand and could lunge down the quarter-mile in the low-14s, with a trap speed of 101 miles per hour. This wasn't a powerplant for beginners.

Pontiac didn't make a dime on Ram Air IV GTO Judges; in fact, it lost close to $1,000 per car. On the über-rare convertible models like this one, it was even more. But the halo effect was priceless. The GTO had, from its earliest days, cut its teeth on venues like Woodward Avenue, and the Ram Air IV–powered Judge was no exception.

With the release of the high-profile Judge, the pressure was on Pontiac to deliver a car that could walk the walk as well as talk the talk. When the hot Pontiac spanked the competition on the street, the word quickly got around, and GTOs of all flavors streamed out of dealerships. As far as Ram Air IV sales, they were a paltry 804 units, but the stormer generated far more ink than the numbers would suggest. Convertibles with the potent engine were really rare; just 24 were built with Turbo Hydro-Matic three-speed automatic transmissions. Even more scarce are four-speed-

equipped Ram Air IV ragtops; just 13 were assembled. Pontiac built just 11 Judge convertibles with the Ram Air IV engine.

The low sales did nothing to convince Pontiac to carry the Ram Air IV over to 1971, making 1970 the last year for the stout powerplant. After this engine, Pontiac would depend on sheer cubic inches to generate power, but even then, output didn't come close to Ram Air IV levels.

Base engine: 400-cubic-inch V-8, 366 horsepower, 445 lbs-ft of torque

Horsepower and torque for this car: 370 horsepower, 445 lbs-ft of torque

Base price: $3,829.00

Price of Ram Air IV engine option: $905.75

Curb weight: 3,700 lbs

Production numbers: 168 Judge convertibles

Number produced with this engine: 11

Part 3

THE DECLINING YEARS

In the 1960s it might have seemed like every emerging generation of car would be faster and more powerful than the last, but as the 1970s got underway almost everyone knew that the American muscle car was on its way out. For one thing the pace of technological development was unsustainable; in the 15 years between the introduction of Oldsmobile's Rocket 88 and Chrysler's 426 Street Hemi, the pushrod overhead-valve V-8 had evolved from a 135-horsepower propulsion device into a fire-breathing 500-horsepower monster. If development had continued at that pace, today's small-block Chevy engine would generate over 25,000 horsepower. Other factors seemed to spell doom for the American performance car too: an aging baby-boom population, exorbitant insurance rates, skyrocketing gasoline prices, and government-mandated pollution controls that would lower compression ratios and castrate horsepower. To make matters worse, beginning in 1972 manufacturers had to give horsepower ratings using the SAE net measuring system, which, while more accurate, also resulted in lower numerical ratings, enhancing the overall sense that American performance cars were going to hell in a hand basket. What's more, it seemed like the United States itself was in that same hand basket. The social situation had started to deteriorate when President John F. Kennedy was assassinated soon after the first GTO rolled off a Pontiac assembly line. Over the next decade the country became embroiled in an unpopular war, cities across the nation erupted in violent protest, and the president of the United States resigned in shame as the result of a botched two-bit burglary. By the time the last of the original muscle cars—Pontiac's SD455 Trans Am and Formula—rolled off the assembly line, the owner needed every one of its 290 SAE net horsepower to outrun the chaos that engulfed the country.

Chapter 36

1971 JAVELIN 401

Law enforcement officials were in a dilemma. perps were driving faster cars than they were driving. Sure, the criminal element always gravitated toward vehicles that could separate them from the scene of the crime at a brisk pace, and most police vehicles were warmed-over production sedans, ideal for pulling over the stray tourist who flagrantly violated any small town's 20-mile-per-hour Main Street speed limit. But the serious offenders, especially in the South, piloted automobiles that had more than a passing acquaintance with hauling ass. The standard police cruiser had zero chance of collaring them.

Alabama State Police officials felt that if they couldn't beat 'em under the rules, then they would change the rules. Pulling a vinyl-roofed AMX from Reinhart AMC in Montgomery, the state police fitted it with a gumball roof light and toured the state, allowing troopers to test the vehicle under real-world conditions. It was well received, but the AMX was rather expensive, so when the Alabama Department of Public Safety ordered its batch of pursuit cars for 1971, they ended up with just 71 1971 Javelin AMXs to be used by the highway patrol. Ten of the vehicles were used as unmarked pursuit cars, though they were fitted with the large tail spoiler like the marked cars. For the 1972 season, 62 Javelins SSTs were ordered. Troopers loved the vehicle because it could run down almost anything. With mild modifications, one police Javelin was clocked at 153 miles per hour. The 401-cubic-inch V-8, factory-rated at 330 horsepower, was bolted to a Borg-Warner three-speed automatic transmission and was durable, able to withstand the abuse of police work. Brakes and suspension, like the engine, were "fleet service" items, a euphemism for heavy-duty.

In the two years that Alabama used the Javelin as a basis for a patrol car, it helped many wanna-be crooks make new friends behind bars. This was the first time that a law-enforcement agency would use a true performance car in this capacity, but as other states saw the success of the program, they emulated Alabama. Chalk one up for the good guys.

Base engine: 360-cubic-inch V-8, 245 horsepower,
Optional engine: 401-cubic-inch V-8, 330 horsepower
Price of engine option: $137
Base price: $3,432
Curb weight: 3,244
Production numbers: 2,054
Number of Javelin AMX 401 police cars produced: 133

Chapter 37

1971 CHEVROLET EL CAMINO SS 454

In 1971, Chevrolet was caught in a vice. Performance enthusiasts were starting to step away from muscle cars due to increasing pressure from insurance companies, so sales were softening. But when the 1971 lineup was green-lighted, performance vehicles were all the rage. So Chevy put a considerable number of its eggs in the high-performance basket. However, tightening emissions regulations were starting to take their toll, resulting in diminished horsepower. The 1971 El Camino SS could still be equipped with a torque-heavy, 454-cubic-inch powerplant, though horsepower levels were down significantly from those available the previous year.

The King-Kong LS6 offered the prior year was a victim of the EPA (it was listed as an available option, though no cars were ever built with the LS6 engine for the 1971 model year), so Chevrolet fitted the 1971 El Camino SS 454 with the LS5 big-block, a cast-iron V-8 with a rated compression ratio of 8.5:1 that generated 365 horsepower with 465 lbs-ft of twist. This was sufficient to fling a '71 El Camino down a drag strip in 14.7 seconds at 96 miles per hour.

Since the El Camino pickup truck was based on the Chevelle passenger car, it shared front bodywork with the automobile, including the single-headlight treatment that appeared in 1971. The interior was pulled from the Chevelle as well, helping to hold down costs. El Camino SS models wore SS badging inside and out, but only the 454-equipped vehicles had engine callouts. Unfortunately, this was the last year that bone-crushing performance was available in the El Camino. The following year the ax came down on muscle cars. Compression ratios plummeted, with predictable results. The 1971 El Camino was truly the last of its breed.

Base engine: 454-cubic-inch V-8, 365 horsepower, 465 lbs-ft of torque

Base price: $2,850.00

Curb weight: 4,050 lbs

Production numbers: 36,942 (V-8)

Number produced with this engine: 9,502

Chapter 38

1971 DODGE CHALLENGER R/T 440-6 "BARN FIND"

The Challenger, Dodge's response to the Mustang and Camaro, debuted in 1970. With its long hood and short deck proportions, it was a classic pony car. But Dodge ensured it came with plenty of grunt; engine choices ranged from very mild to very wild. While much of the ink was spilled on the 426 Hemi, savvy buyers knew that if they wanted a reliable, powerful engine that didn't require a tune-up every weekend, the 440 was the way to go. Unlike the 1970 Challenger line, Dodge wouldn't offer a Challenger convertible for 1971. In its sophomore year, Dodge's E-body only came as a coupe.

This 1971 Challenger R/T features the big RB-block 440 topped with the famous Six-Pak induction system, a fancy name for three two-barrel carburetors. Running on the center carb most of the time, mashing the gas pedal opened the end carbs, allowing a *lot* of fuel to fill the combustion chambers, with the expected spectacular results.

Big engines are expected to deliver big performance, and the 1971 Challenger R/T 440-6 didn't disappoint. It could cover the quarter-mile in 13.4 seconds while flashing through the lights at 107 miles per hour. This is a stylish machine that could scare the wits out of you. Especially when trying to stop from that speed. But Dodge didn't make the Challenger R/T to stop.

This example is what all of us dream about—an unmolested original barn find. With its four-speed manual transmission, Shaker hood scoop, and vinyl top, it begs to be given its head. Truly original muscle cars are becoming rarer, thus increasing the worth of the unrestored examples like this.

Base engine: 383-cubic-inch V-8, 250 horsepower (SAE net), 325 lbs-ft of torque (SAE net)

Horsepower and torque for this car: 385 horsepower (SAE gross), 490 lbs-ft of torque (SAE gross)

Base price: $3,273.00

Curb weight: 3,495 lbs

Production numbers: 3,814

Number produced with this engine: 250

1971 DODGE CHALLENGER R/T 440-6

Chapter 39

1971 DODGE CHARGER R/T 426 HEMI AND 440 MAGNUM

The end of the muscle car line was in view when these 1971 Charger R/T models were built. The rarest versions were those equipped with the last of the mighty Hemi engines. The Hemi Orange car with white top shown here was the first of 63 Hemi-powered Chargers built for the 1971 model year, and the Hemi Orange car with the black top was the second Hemi off the line. The first car, an SE version, features every option Chrysler offered, including a sunroof and Dictaphone. The second vehicle was used in Dodge's dealer brochure, igniting auto lust in young hearts coast to coast. Unfortunately, few young hearts could afford the $4,000-plus needed to put a Hemi-powered Charger in their garages.

The long, low, new-for-'71 body traded the boxiness of the previous generation of Chargers for sensuous curves. Unlike most engines in 1971, the 426 Hemi retained its 425-horsepower rating. Two transmissions were bolted to the back of the block: the four-speed manual featured in car number two (30 built), and the Torqueflite three-speed automatic featured in car number one (33 built).

While the bulk of enthusiast ink was spilled on the outrageous Hemi engine, the vast bulk of Charger R/Ts built in 1971 came with the very capable 440-cubic-inch engine. Available in two flavors—single four-barrel Magnum and triple two-barrel Six-Pack—it cranked out 370 ponies with the solo carb and 385 horses with the "Six-Pak" setup. The yellow car shown here features the Magnum version of the engine.

Motor Trend magazine flogged a Hemi-equipped Super Bee, the Charger R/T's cousin, and came up with a quarter-mile time of 13.73 seconds at 104 miles per hour. Remember, we're talking a two-ton street car on street tires. In 1971. The

Charger R/T came with heavy-duty Rallye suspension, heavy-duty brakes and shock absorbers, and even a functional Ramcharger hood scoop on Hemi models. The 1971 Charger R/T Hemi spoke in a bold visual language, but it had the cojones to back up the hype.

Base engine: 440-cubic-inch V-8, 370 horsepower, 480 lbs-ft of torque

Horsepower and torque for this car: 426-cubic-inch V-8, 425 horsepower, 490 lbs-ft of torque

Base price: $3,777.00

Price of Hemi engine option: $707.00

Curb weight: 3,685 lbs

Production numbers: 3,118

Number produced with 426 Hemi engine: 63

1971 DODGE CHARGER

Chapter 40

1971 DODGE CHARGER SUPER BEE

When the newly restyled Charger hit the street in 1971, the Super Bee had been demoted from a free-standing model to an option package on the Charger.

The basic Super Bee formula remained the same: the highest possible performance at the lowest possible cost. The standard 383 engine was bulletproof and battle tested, an ideal powerplant for a vehicle destined to lead a harsh life. Customers who wanted more of everything usually popped for the 440-cubic-inch mill, a torque monster that could wreath a car in tire smoke without breaking a sweat. For buyers who had to have top-shelf performance, the 426 Hemi was still available, ready to threaten driveline components and empty fuel tanks on command.

Regardless of the engine under the huge hood, the Super Bee was a visually intimidating piece of machinery. With its flowing lines, full-width grill, and aggressive rumble, most sane people would think twice before challenging this one-year-only option package. Dodge held down costs by using a bench seat and a floor-mounted three-speed manual transmission as standard equipment. For the customer who had a pile of green burning a hole in his or her pocket, the options list was practically endless. Buyers chasing low E.T.'s found that the drag strip could be put into the mirror in just 13.7 seconds at 104 miles per hour if a Hemi resided under the hood.

Unfortunately, the Super Bee was a victim of the collapsing muscle car market. Its last year would be 1971, as it would be for the 426 Hemi engine. Dodge, like all manufacturers, closely followed their dealers' weekly sales reports, and it didn't take a rocket scientist to see that high-powered muscle cars were collecting dust on dealer lots. Quick as a power shift, they pulled the plug on the Super Bee.

Base engine: 383-cubic-inch V-8, single four-barrel, 300 horsepower, 410 lbs-ft of torque

Optional engines: 440-cubic-inch V-8, single four-barrel, 375 horsepower, 480 lbs-ft of torque; 440-cubic-inch V-8, 3x2-barrel, 390 horsepower, 490 lbs-ft of torque; 426-cubic-inch V-8, 2x4-barrel, 425 horsepower, 480 lbs-ft of torque

Base price: $3,271.00

Curb weight: 4,050 lbs

Production numbers: 5,054

1971 DODGE CHARGER SUPER BEE

Chapter 41

1971 OLDSMOBILE 4-4-2 W-30

While Oldsmobile isn't the first brand that comes up when the discussion turns to classic muscle cars, ignoring the potent 4-4-2 would be a serious omission. Even in 1971, when it was clear to everyone that performance cars were quickly becoming yesterday's news, the 4-4-2 still generated enough performance to scare the horses. Add the W-30 option, and the potential for antisocial behavior ratcheted up another notch.

In 1971, GM lowered engine compression ratios in an attempt to satisfy emissions regulations, and the performance of the 4-4-2 W-30 suffered as a result. Dish-topped pistons brought the compression ratio down to 8.5:1, allowing the muscle car to run on regular leaded fuel. The 455 cubic inches still delivered massive torque, however, and on the street, torque rules. Even with diminished raw horsepower, the big engine could hurl the 4-4-2 W-30 to 60 miles per hour in just 6.5 seconds. The drag strip was a user-friendly place for the muscular Olds, which could still travel the quarter-mile in 14.8 seconds at 98 miles per hour. A low-restriction air cleaner, high-flow exhaust system, aluminum intake manifold, and functional cold-air intake in the hood helped the W-30 to generate more-than-adequate power. The engines were blueprinted at the factory to help extract every possible pony. Oldsmobile even fit the intake and exhaust valves with rotators to prevent hot spots on the valve faces that might affect combustion.

Being an Oldsmobile meant that the 4-4-2 W-30, regardless of its brutal acceleration, was a pleasure to drive.

Base engine: 455-cubic-inch V-8, 340 horsepower, 370 lbs-ft of torque

Optional engine, W-30: 455-cubic-inch V-8, 350 horsepower, 460 lbs-ft of torque

Base price: $4,000.00

Price of W-30 option: $347.56

Curb weight: 3,620 lbs

Production numbers: 920 (total 4-4-2 W-30)

Number produced with this engine: 810

1971 OLDSMOBILE 4-4-2 W-30

Chapter 42

1971 PLYMOUTH HEMI 'CUDA

By 1971, Plymouth could see the writing on the wall. Performance, in the form of tire-smoking, fuel-guzzling muscle cars, was about to be referred to in the past tense. But before the curtain could drop on socially irresponsible fun, the E-body 'Cuda returned in its sophomore year still full of brash horsepower and a bad attitude. The 426 Hemi was about to be ushered off of the stage, but not without a fight. Granted, the Elephant wasn't selling in sufficient numbers to put any money in Plymouth's coffers, but the halo effect from the monster engine settled on the entire range of Barracudas.

A mild restyling of the front grille and the addition of front fender gills made the 'Cuda visually different from its predecessor. Huge optional vinyl graphics could be affixed, raising the stand-out quotient considerably. Of course, one didn't buy a Hemi 'Cuda to blend in.

The 115 buyers who were willing to ante up $883.90 for the Hemi option alone got a drive to remember. Able to lunge down the quarter-mile in just 14 seconds at 102 miles per hour, the biggest problem was finding traction. With 425 horsepower and a tidal wave of torque, there wasn't a street tire made that could effectively get the power down. Granted, build quality could be spotty; rattling door glass and misaligned body panels were part of the vehicle's charm.

But charm went out the window when the accelerator was slammed down. Part of the appeal of any muscle car is the whole-body experience; with the pedal down, the sounds, vibration, smells (Is that my clutch?), blurring scenery, and growing pressure on the back added up to an intoxicating brew. Few automobiles could touch the Hemi 'Cuda for sensory immersion.

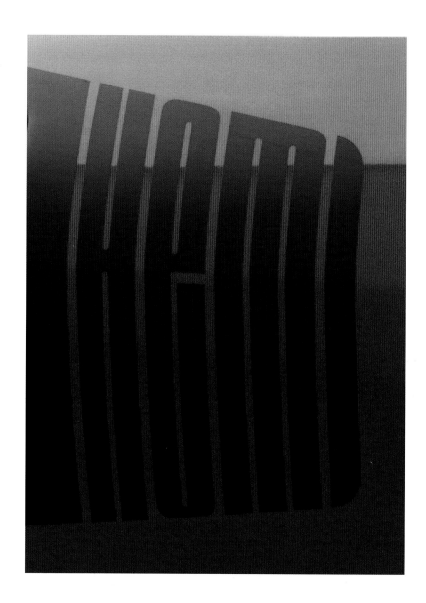

Base engine: 426-cubic-inch V-8, 425 horsepower, 490 lbs-ft of torque

Base price: $4,040

Curb weight: 3,500 lbs

Production numbers: 108 hardtops, 7 convertibles

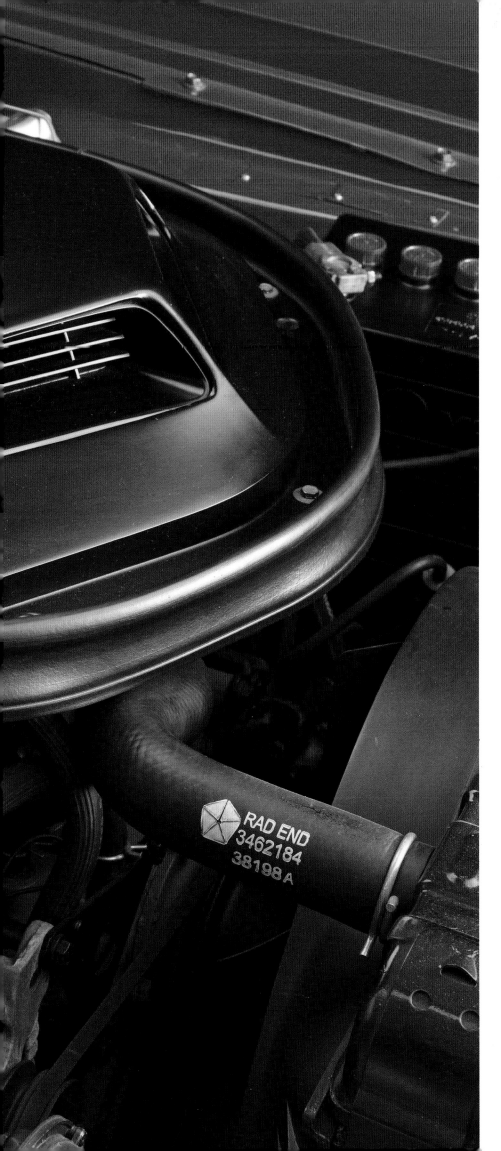

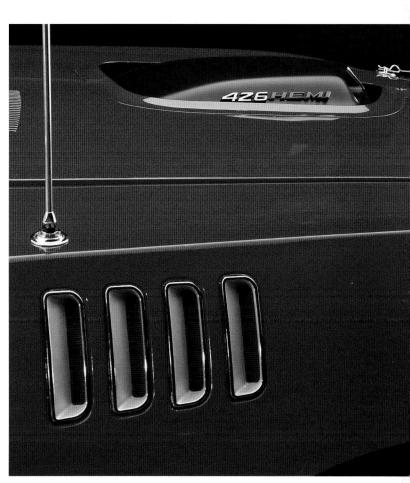

1971 PLYMOUTH HEMI 'CUDA

Chapter 43

1971 PLYMOUTH ROAD RUNNER HEMI

One of the cardinal rules when performing on stage is that you should always leave the audience wanting more. Plymouth followed that advice with the 1971 Road Runner, since it was something of a bookend model. It was the first year for a new body style and the last year for the famed 426 Hemi engine. For hard-core performance enthusiasts, it was time to pay up or shut up. Unfortunately, too many people sat on their wallets.

The body was based on the Satellite and was far more flowing and swoopy than in years prior. However, the lack of a convertible saddened the sun worshipers. A huge bumper encircled the grille, while indentations on the hood carried engine call-outs. The Road Runner was available with four different engines: a 383-cubic-inch base engine, two optional 440s, and the 426 Hemi. Built in surprisingly low numbers (55), the Road Runner Hemi was still rated at 425 horsepower, with the torque-O-meter reading 490 lbs-ft. With that kind of grunt, the drag strip could be dispatched in the low-13-second range, and trap speeds were comfortably in the triple-digit realm.

Yet performance, at least in the brute muscle car sense, was no longer a gleam in most customers' eyes. The insurance companies were on their last nerve regarding hot cars and accidents, and with the jacking up of rates, insurance premiums could conceivably be higher than the monthly vehicle payment. Most buyers didn't want the hassle, and with the one-two punch of higher fuel prices and declining power outputs, muscle cars were doomed. But at least Plymouth pulled its fierce Hemi while it still had its bite. Nobody wanted a toothless Hemi. Those 55 buyers, in hindsight, were very smart. Who would have thought a Hemi would be worth a dime. Who indeed?

Base engine: 383-cubic-inch V-8, 300 horsepower, 410 lbs-ft of torque

Optional engines: 340-cubic-inch V-8, 275 horsepower, 340 lbs-ft of torque;

440-cubic-inch V-8, 385 horsepower, 490 lbs-ft of torque;

426-cubic-inch V-8, 425 horsepower, 490 lbs-ft of torque

Base price: $3,147

Price of Hemi engine option: $884

Curb weight: 3,640 lbs

Production numbers: 14,218

Number produced with this engine: 55

1971 PLYMOUTH ROAD RUNNER HEMI

Chapter 44

1971 PLYMOUTH GTX 440

The GTX and the Road Runner were like twins, only not. While the Road Runner and the GTX were both based on the intermediate Satellite, the two nameplates took different paths on the road to performance. From its inception, the Road Runner was essentially a stripper muscle car, while the GTX exuded an upscale look and feel. The interior was awash in genuine simulated-wood-grain plastic, and high-back bucket seats were a comfortable touch. With the adoption of the new platform, the GTX grew some curves, looking more like a styled vehicle than a mere repository for huge engines. Plymouth called the new design "Fuselage Styling," whatever that meant.

The $3,733 GTX wasn't the cheapest midsize muscle car in the Plymouth lineup; that trophy belonged to the Road Runner. The GTX pursued a customer who wanted a few more creature comforts while retaining retina-crushing performance. Not exactly a lightweight vehicle at 3,675 lbs, the GTX was still a fast car in 1971. The Super Commando 440-cubic-inch engine belted out 370 horsepower, sufficient to hurl the GTX down the drag strip in 14.9 seconds at 95.4 miles per hour. The 440's massive torque worked to whip the speedometer needle to 60 miles per hour in just 6.5 ticks of the second hand. Standard on the GTX were heavy-duty underpinnings and functional dual exhaust, the better to annoy mere pedestrians. The GTX enjoyed a three-inch-wider track than the prior year's model, aiding in handling. Customers were starting to expect a vehicle, yes, even a muscle car, to go around a corner without embarrassing itself. Yet nobody was under any illusions that the GTX wasn't a straight-line muscle car.

Like prior years, the GTX wasn't a big seller, with only 2,538 being built with the base 440-4 engine. Just 135 were equipped with the 440 Six-Pak.

Base engine: 440-cubic-inch V-8, 370 horsepower, 480 lbs-ft of torque

Optional engine: 440-cubic-inch V-8, 3x2 barrel, 385 horsepower, 490 lbs-ft of torque; 426-cubic-inch Hemi V-8, 425 horsepower, 490 lbs-ft of torque

Base price: $3,800

Curb weight: 4,022

Production numbers: 2,942—total

Number produced with this engine: 135

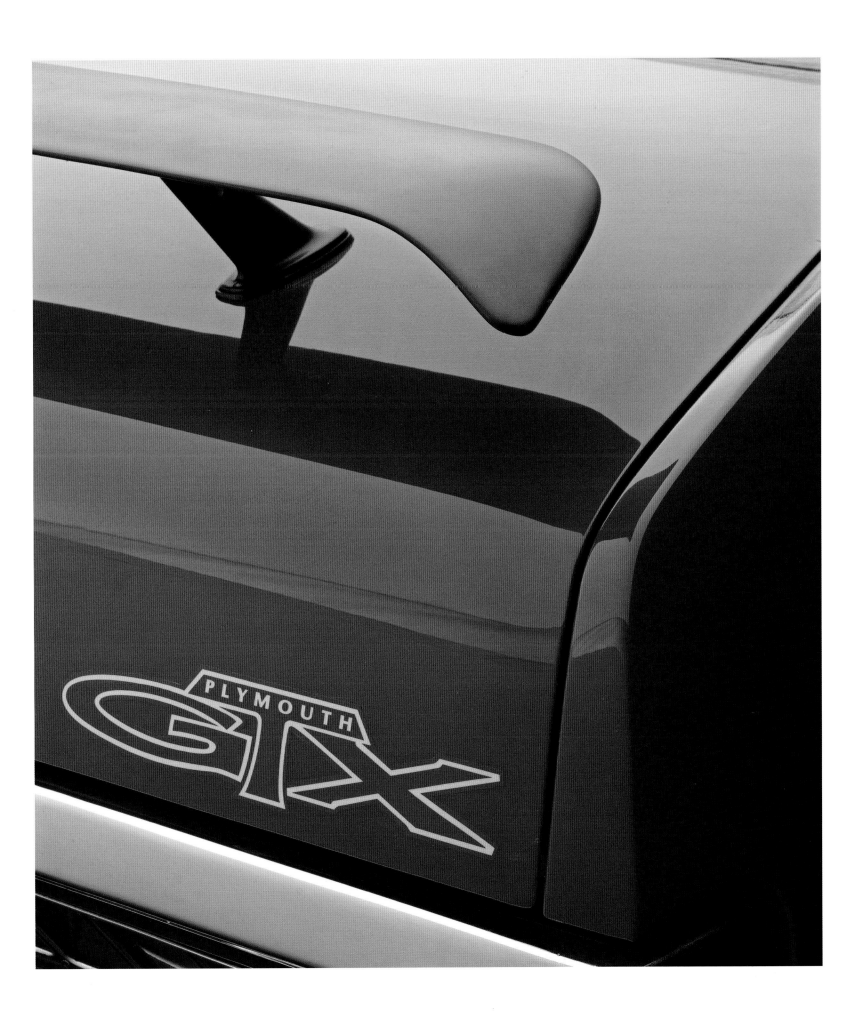

1971 PLYMOUTH GTX 440

Chapter 45

1972 OLDSMOBILE HURST/OLDS CONVERTIBLE

It took an accident for the Hurst/Olds to get onto the Indianapolis Motor Speedway. During the 1971 Indy 500 race, the pace car, a Dodge Challenger, overshot the track exit on the final pace lap and struck the press box. A number of members of the Fourth Estate were tossed about, leaving no small amount of egg on Dodge's face. For the 1972 race, no manufacturer wanted to chance another PR disaster, so George Hurst stepped up and said that his company would provide the vehicles. It was the first time that a non-manufacturer supplied the pace vehicles for the Indy 500.

For the track, 76 Oldsmobiles were provided: 42 convertibles, 27 coupes, 6 station wagons, and 1 sedan. Part of the reason manufacturers had been pacing the race was for the exposure, and Hurst was no different. He had partnered with Oldsmobile a number of years before, so it was a no-brainer for the two to team up for the pace car project. Oldsmobile benefited from its car being the basis for the Hurst/Olds, and that advantage was pressed with the release of "civilian" versions of the track cars.

These were all virtually identical, with 455-cubic-inch engines bolted to Turbo Hydramatic 400 three-speed automatic transmissions. Of course, being a Hurst endeavor, every car had a Hurst Dual-Gate shifter. It was found that the Rallye suspension, FE2, provided a good mixture of grip and good manners. To keep engine rpm low during highway cruising, a 3.23:1 rear axle ratio was used. Some H/Os were fitted with W-30 packages, including red plastic inner fender liners. W-30–equipped cars were fitted with 3.42:1 rear axle ratios.

Finished in the Hurst traditional colors of Cameo White with Hurst Gold accents, the Hurst/Olds was a handsome and head-turning machine, from a time when how a car looked was almost as important as how fast it ran.

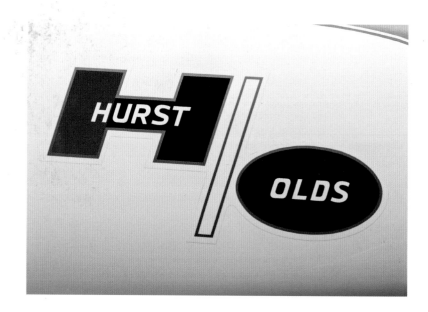

Base engine: 455-cubic-inch V-8, 270 horsepower (SAE net), 370 lbs-ft of torque (SAE net)

Optional engine: W-30, 455-cubic-inch V-8, 300 horsepower (SAE net), 410 lbs-ft of torque (SAE net)

Base price: $2,972.00

Price of W-30 option: $414.60

Curb weight: 3,614 lbs

Production numbers: 130 convertibles, 499 coupes

Chapter 46

1973 PONTIAC TRANS AM SUPER DUTY

It was over. Kaput. The muscle car was dead and buried. It was common knowledge that insurance companies, emissions regulations, and paltry sales had doomed the performance car to history. Then *this* car hit the scene. With power not seen in years, in a vehicle that everyone had written off as a pony car with delusions of grandeur instead of a serious muscle car, Pontiac's Super Duty Trans Am screamed onto the road like Berserker headed for Valhalla.

The Trans Am was a tough-looking car, with its Endura front bumper, taut sheet metal, and low, wide stance. Stuff the Super Duty 455 engine under the hood, plaster the "screaming chicken" decal on top of it, fire it up, and go trolling for Corvettes. Pontiac had considerable experience with racing engines, and it brought this knowledge to bear in developing the Super Duty 455. Reinforced block with extra webbing, forged connecting rods, aluminum pistons, four-bolt main bearing caps—the list of race-ready components was as long as your arm. This was essentially a race engine detuned to run on the street. It even had provisions for a dry-sump lubrication system.

The heads were works of art. Though the ports were smaller than on Ram Air engines, they were shaped to maximize the velocity of the fuel-air charge, especially at low- and midrange engine speeds, which is where the Super Duty lived. It had a redline of just 5,700 rpm, but with the tidal wave of torque low in the tach's range, there was no need to thrash the engine to kick someone's butt.

An accommodation of the low-octane swill that passed for pump gas at the time, the compression ratio of 8.4:1 was

nothing spectacular, but when all the go-fast goodies were bolted together, the Super Duty could propel a Trans Am down the quarter-mile in just 13.54 seconds at 104.29 miles per hour. Nothing in 1973 could touch it, and few cars before '73 could either.

Base engine: 455-cubic-inch V-8, 250 horsepower (SAE net),
370 lbs-ft of torque (SAE net)
Horsepower and torque for this car: 290 horsepower, 390 lbs-ft of torque
Base price: $4,204.00
Price of SD engine option: $521.00
Curb weight: 3,504 lbs
Production numbers: 4,802
Number produced with this engine: 252

1973 PONTIAC TRANS AM SUPER DUTY

Chapter 47

1974 PONTIAC TRANS AM SUPER DUTY 455

In its second and last year, the Trans Am Super Duty 455 had already earned a legendary reputation. Pontiac, complying with federal regulations requiring real bumpers on the front of a car for 1974, had redesigned the nose of the Trans Am. The result earned mixed reviews, but nobody was complaining about the locomotive-grade power that the Super Duty 455 engine dished out. The staggering performance of the 1973 Super Duty had enthusiasts heading to Pontiac showrooms to check out the '74 version, and sales were considerably better the second time around.

The 1974 Trans Am was a year of lasts, including the last Super Duty 455 and the last true dual exhausts. Catalytic converters would appear for the 1975 model year, as unleaded fuel flowed onto the scene. Regular Trans Ams suffered with numerically lower rear axle ratios, but the Super Duty 455 could still be had with an aggressive 3.42:1 ratio. Pontiac saw that the new radial tires could have a positive influence on vehicle dynamics, and the division installed radials as the standard tires on most of its models in 1974. When these tires combined with Pontiac's traditional emphasis on handling, the '74 Trans Am could challenge the Corvette on a slalom track.

At a drag strip, the Trans Am Super Duty 455 would put a 1974 Corvette on the trailer. Covering the quarter-mile in just 13.5 seconds at 104 miles per hour, the Super Duty 455 was the top dog in a shrinking field. The muscle car crowd ate it up, but it was inevitable that the good times couldn't last. Compression ratios would continue to fall, dragging performance with them.

As the 1970s wore on, performance would be measured in cubic inches of graphics covering the sheet metal rather than in quarter-mile times. But for a brief time, the Super Duty 455 ruled the roost. It went out on a very high note.

Base engine: 400-cubic-inch V-8, 225 horsepower, 330 lbs-ft of torque

Optional engines: 455-cubic-inch V-8, 250 horsepower, 380 lbs-ft of torque;
(Super Duty) 455-cubic-inch V-8, 290 horsepower, 395 lbs-ft of torque

Base price: $4,446.00

Price of SD engine option: $578.00

Curb weight: 3,655 lbs

Production numbers: 10,255

Number produced with this engine: 943

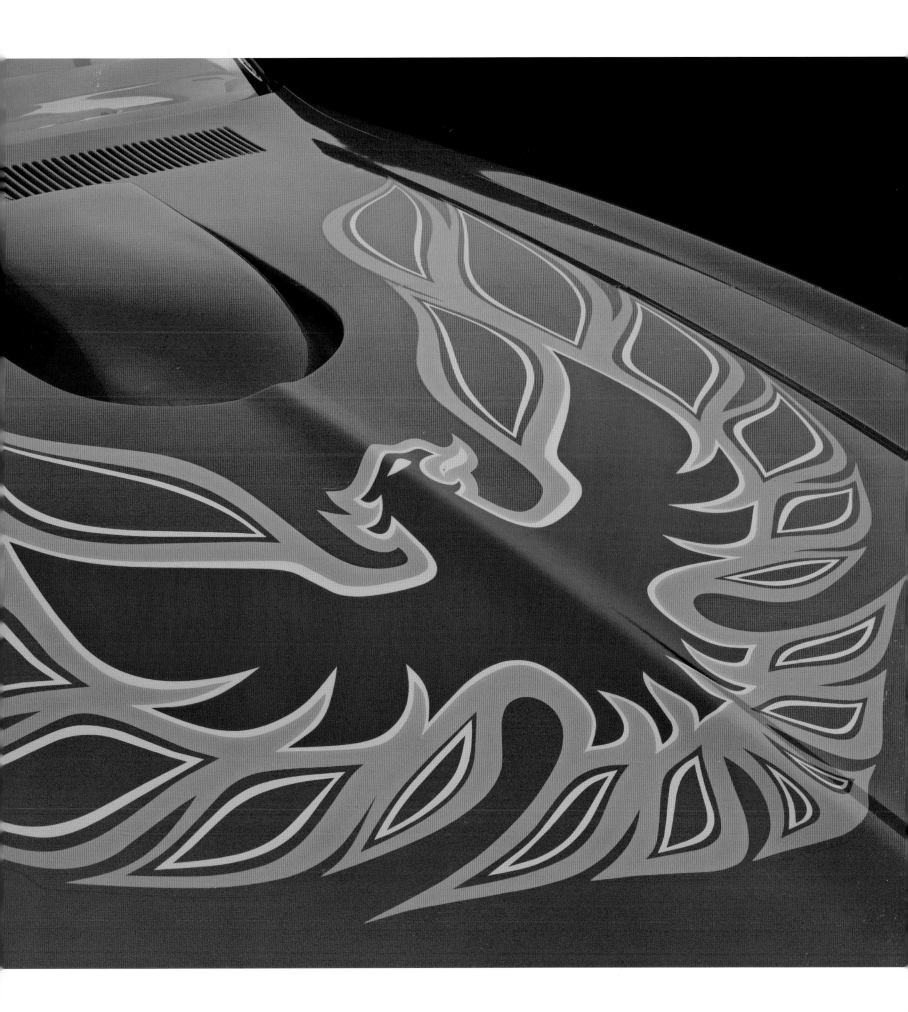

1974 PONTIAC TRANS AM SUPER DUTY 455

INDEX